THE
STEP-UP
MINDSET
FOR NEW
MANAGERS

MARGO
MANNING

The Step-Up Mindset for New Managers

First published in 2016 by

Panoma Press Ltd
48 St Vincent Drive, St Albans, Herts, AL1 5SJ, UK
info@panomapress.com
www.panomapress.com

Book design and layout by Neil Coe.

Printed on acid-free paper from managed forests.

ISBN 978-1-784520-91-5

The right of Margo Manning to be identified as the author of this work has been asserted in accordance with sections 77 and 78 of the Copyright, Designs and Patents Act 1988.

A CIP catalogue record for this book is available from the British Library.

This book is available online and in bookstores.

Dedicated to Phil and Galloway who never
question and always support.

TESTIMONIALS

"It is rare for a Leadership and Management Coach and Mentor to come along who has an in-depth understanding and empathy for the most junior to the most senior managers. Margo does just that: she has a crystal clear knowledge of the issues and concerns managers face. I suspect part of the reason for this is Margo continues to work with junior staff to ensure that she gets a 360 degree picture of the environment that managers are working within.

In this book, Margo takes the mystery and fog out of management for first time managers. She gives them a book that embraces not just the practical skills, but also behaviour and attitude alignment. She translates this into an easy read with practical exercises and reflections. I will be purchasing this book for all my first time managers, and some of my more senior managers who could also learn from it."

**Sharron Clow, Director of HR and Legacy,
Legacy Strategies Limited**

"As a very experienced manager, this book introduced me to new concepts and reminded me to reinforce my management foundations."

Tony Falltrick, Service Operations Manager

"New within a management role, this book was pivotal in turning around my weaknesses into strengths."

Colin Fulcher, Strategic Project Manager, Argyll & Bute Council

"An excellent place to start for those wanting to take their first steps onto the management ladder."

James Messenger, Section QS

"An essential handbook for managers seeking an insightful and structured route to successful leadership and career progression."

Carrie Byrne, Web and Media Designer

ACKNOWLEDGMENTS

Carrie Byrne for the great sugar-free home baking; and of course for helping me to filter my thoughts without filtering the enthusiasm for this book.

Tony 'Montana' Falltrick for your honest review.

Colin Fulcher, who always has a positive outlook and helped tremendously with your feedback.

James Messenger – thank you for your red pen marking. Your feedback was invaluable.

Jayne D'Souza who stayed through it all, rolled her eyes and laughed! You are the nuts and bolts.

Jonathan Ward-Brown, Sarah Blackburn, Stuart Crump, Chris Kassell and Warren Midgley - thank you.

Sharron Clow, one in a million!

Dawn Burnett for being you and never putting down my latest fad – and you have seen a few come and go.

Rachel 'The Boff' Lambert, for knowing you are there.

CONTENTS

INTRODUCTION

This book is written for new managers who want, need or wish to change their outcomes; for those who want a different ending to their current story; for those who want to make the 'Step-Up' to something new, more exciting and rewarding. It is for those who want or are required to step-up their performance in preparation for a new role, promotion, or even enhance their performance within their current role, and those who are ready to make changes to their skill-set, their behaviour and their attitude.

Think about what would be different if you knew where you really wanted to be. Not just a vague thought or wish, but a solid knowing. It could be promotion, or to be better at..., or "Wouldn't it be great if I earned more money?"

What if you had clear goals, objectives, vision and the toolkit firstly to know what you want and secondly how to achieve your success? Can you imagine how this would feel?

You do not have to: this book will give you the tools to transition this from your imagination to a realistic goal. It will assist you on the start of your managerial career, or if you're in an existing role, it will remind you of what you should be doing and how to do it. It will help break the bad habits.

This book will take you from "I know I should be doing *something* better or *something* different" to "I know where I am going with work (and possibly your personal life), what my motivation is, what I need to be doing to get there and how I need to be feeling in order to reach this". You can reach this by working through the book and completing the exercises at the end of the relevant chapters.

Now stop, take a big breath and know this is the book for you. With an investment of your time and thoughts, you are about to start a journey that will have a greater impact on your life than you can imagine. Know that taking time to breathe and reflect will pay dividends on your return. You will be covering many of the key skills required to become a successful manager whilst also reflecting on your own attitude and behaviour.

Take your time to read through this book. Ensure that you complete the 'Reflection and Actions' section at the end of each chapter. This will drive your success forward on your roadmap and Step-Up mindset change, resulting in a positive long term impact on your goals.

Let's get started...

CHAPTER 1
THE MANAGER'S DNA

Managers come in many shapes and sizes, many styles, many levels of experience and many levels of adequacy, from the great to the bland to the downright awful.

The *great* leaders will have taken you from a starting point to somewhere better. They have led you through lapses in judgment and confidence to a grounded safe place; through the unknown to the clearing; they have supported you when you were having personal difficulties, and more. You remember them fondly, like the schoolteacher who believed in you.

The *bland* leaders…I can't quite remember what they did or who they were. Sorry.

Then there are the *downright awful* leaders who have taken you from heady heights, where you were confident in your abilities, performing, enjoying your job (and therefore life was generally good), to a place where you question yourself, double and triple checking your work, highlighting your every mistake, and you dread going into work.

Why is there such a disparity between the great, the bland and the downright awful managers?

DISPARATE MANAGERS

Nature or nurture

People are not born leaders and so it must be nurture winning (or losing) over nature. And here lies the problem with managers. There is no one size fits all, and sadly that means there is no prescriptive solution for the downright awful managers and leaders.

A lot of managers will have worked their way through the 'tools': starting at a junior position, carrying out a good job at that level, being promoted to a management position and possibly not doing as well as had been hoped. How well were these individuals nurtured, developed and supported? What recognition have they received? Where was *their* great manager supporting and developing them?

It is not rocket science, so why is it people are surprised when great technical workers sometime make awful managers?

One reason for this is they haven't been given the tools to manage their staff or situations. They do not have the tools to manage themselves, let alone recognise and manage underperformers within their team, communicate effectively, manage objectives and deadlines, and let's not go near delegation! Good grief, how many times have you heard managers moan, "I am working all the hours"; "I have no time to do anything"; "I am missing deadlines" and so forth? If only they shared the workload with their team, everyone, including they themselves, would be happier.

If only they had the Step-Up Mindset.

The Step-Up Mindset will progress you to a place that gives you confidence to think and behave as a manager in your delivery, allowing you to manage not only yourself, but also your team and their tasks, and let us not forget your manager.

A GREAT MANAGER'S ATTRIBUTES

A great manager has several positive attributes that include:

Effective communicator

A great manager knows which style to adopt for each individual scenario. They tailor their communication and management style to get the best out of the individuals within their team as well as doing what is best for the business. They recognise that one size does not fit all and communicate in a way that is effective and motivating to their team, colleagues, peers, managers, clients and others, adapting their language for their audience. They are authentic with their communication.

Goal driven

A great manager knows where they are going and how to take along the team without the need to push and shove. They use the 'TRUSTed' format to have clarity and structure understanding and know the goals required for success, then communicate these goals with their team and with key contacts, getting buy-in from all.

Results focused

Success must be measured. The results are tangible, provided in black and white. A great manager takes time to consider the outcomes and the meaning of the results, and adjusts and rewards accordingly.

Responsive

A great manager is responsive to others' needs, not in a knee jerk manner, but in a calm, thought-through and timely manner. They will come back with a response even when it might not be what you want to hear, or one the manager wants to give.

Balanced

A great manager knows how to apply the Law of Balance to all aspects of their working (and personal) life, and works with their team to assign and support balance.

Transparency

A great manager understands there are areas of business that they are unable to share: HR related, bonuses, salaries, etc. With the areas that can be shared, they are open and honest, and share them with all of the team where applicable. They share their concerns and issues with the team as well as their successes.

Fairness

A great manager will treat each member of the team fairly as individuals, without favouritism.

Trustworthy

A great manager will be honest with good news and feedback as well as constructive criticism. The team will know that what the manager is saying is true at the time of the message. The manager will not try and fudge or hide negative news; they will face it and look for appropriate solutions.

Approachable

A great manager will give their team the confidence to approach them with bad news as well as good news without fear of reprisal. This manager will give their team members the confidence to approach with issues and solutions, knowing they will be listened to.

Learning environment

A great manager will create a learning environment with calculated risks. The team will be allowed to work within agreed parameters and learn from their mistakes without fear of blame. When issues arise, a great manager will look at what went wrong and work with the team to learn lessons and implement resolutions without finger pointing.

All of the above attributes come down to focus – being able to articulate what success looks like and inspire attitudes and behaviours whilst ensuring the required skill sets are in place to deliver.

Throughout the course of this book you will identify and develop these attributes.

MANAGERS' REPUTATION AND BRAND

Your reputation far exceeds your marketing reach

Many companies will allocate a large part of their budget on advertising and marketing, looking to ensure that their brand is exactly aligned to their wants and wishes.

Individuals will allocate very little effort and time to ensuring that their brand is aligned to their own wants, needs and wishes. If anything, it is no more than a passing thought.

Time, effort, money, advertising and marketing, if used wisely, will work towards the company's and individual's reputation and brand, but many people seem to forget that your *reputation far exceeds your marketing reach*. By that, I mean your reputation is grown over time. It is built through a series of interactions with others, promises delivered or broken, trust and respect that you command or lose – every interaction with someone else steers your reputation and brand for better or worse.

Your brand is not what you believe you are delivering: it is what is being received by others. It is built on others' perceptions, and whilst you have a great influence over it, ultimately you cannot control it.

The delusional

Many years ago I worked with a manager who I would categorise in the 'delusional' slot. What I (and many others) received from this manager was a short tempered communication style, unrealistic commands, lots of mood swings, flighty favouritism and ingratitude. This was in complete contrast to what he believed his reputation and brand to be. He believed that his communication was delivering a firm and yet fair approach, being level-headed and open. He claimed he didn't want to make friends, he just wanted others' respect.

There was a real disconnect between what he perceived to be true and what was actually true. He was disliked, disrespected and delusional.

What did this manager's management style mean to his reputation?

You do the maths! He felt and vocalised that he was a fair manager, but he had four direct reports with a team of 30 talking badly of him. What is one manager's positive marketing reach versus 30 negative comments?

This is a real and long lasting lesson on delusional management! Do not take for granted that you are managing your reputation: ask for feedback.

The jobsworth

On a separate occasion I worked with the jobsworth. This lady was good at what she did, but when asked to do something outside her role or process, she flatly refused. Her response was, "That is not what I get paid for" or "We don't do it that way, and we are not about to start now". She thought that she was a specialist in her area, she had a niche position within the company and was indispensable within the role. She believed her reputation was that of someone who was dependable (she was right – you could always depend on her not to be helpful), delivering a good standard each and every time.

If you asked others what her reputation and brand represented, you would receive replies like: "She's unhelpful"; "She is difficult to work with"; "She's a jobsworth"; "She is inflexible". As a result, her role never grew or changed whilst the business around her was changing.

A couple of years later, whilst I was working for another company, this lady was interviewed for a role within my new company. The interviewer, realising that we had worked together, asked me for my opinion on her. I gave an honest opinion that she was good at what she did if she felt it was part of her role and on her job spec, but she didn't extend herself or her role, and for me she was a jobsworth. On this occasion her reputation far exceeded her marketing (CV) reach. Her progression within the interview process was terminated.

One of the most damaging parts of this story is that if she had had a strong and worthwhile manager who was a good communicator, they would have been able to steer her in the right direction. They could have motivated and influenced her attitude towards being more flexible and helpful, and I genuinely believe she would have been a more contented individual within her role and her reputation would have been enhanced.

However, I was not prepared to put my neck or reputation on the line to find out if this was the case.

Either feed their delusions or their facts

Your confidence as a manager in feeding back to someone who has a blind spot is a critical skill. It effectively allows you to manage people like the cases above in a more effective manner. That can only benefit all those involved.

Communication is vital to your success and that of your team, and of course the company. In the first case study the manager completely misjudged his reputation, and in the second case study you saw the jobsworth in action. Whilst she was doing a good job, she was not delivering on what needed to happen and her reputation was very disconnected from what she believed.

A strong manager was needed in both cases: a manager who was assertive and inclusive, had the confidence and a good understanding, and cared what was going on around them and their teams. Such a manager could have potentially turned the individuals and their reputations around. In both cases, I find it hard to believe that the managers did not know of the unrest and the gossip caused by their direct reports, and yet there was no action taken. I felt this reflected badly on the managers.

Ignorance

Being ignorant of your reputation and that of your company is no excuse. Planning to change your reputation through marketing alone doesn't work. Brand and reputation are based on repeated actions, good or bad.

CHAPTER REFLECTION AND ACTION – OWN YOUR REPUTATION

You cannot buy your reputation through marketing or advertising, you must work towards it and earn it. It must be part of you. You have to be authentic and believe in what you are sharing: trying to gain a brand that is in complete contrast to your natural self will not be sustainable. the truth will always come out.

It is imperative that you source what other are saying about you. This is not a 'go to the people I like and who like me in order to gain fantastic feedback' exercise, neither is it a 'go to the Moaning Minnie's of this world' exercise. It is about balance.

Aim to get a real feel for your reputation by asking various people. You cannot guess or assume with regards to your reputation and brand. It is important that you know what has been received and perceived by others in order for you to start putting out the correct communications. Ask clients, your manager, your team, and ensure that you ask those who will tell you both the good and the areas for improvement.

A manager's reputation prior to working within a team can often lay the foundation to a great or not so good relationship. Ensure your reputation works for you, or if you are new to this, your brand entry is on track.

1. What questions would I want to ask to gain feedback on my reputation?

2. Which five people would I ask?

3. What will I do with the feedback?

Remember: your reputation far exceeds your marketing reach.

CHAPTER 2
THE STEP-UP MINDSET

Your mindset is your roadmap to success. Unfortunately, a wrong or disjointed mindset can also be your roadmap to disappointment. Depending upon your mindset, at any given time it will have a major impact on your outcomes.

A good mindset produces a great attitude which produces great behaviour that will normally result in great outcomes. The other side of the same coin is a bad mindset, which will produce a negative attitude that produces detrimental behaviour and usually toxic outcomes.

Start designing the roadmap that will lead to your success.

YOUR RESOURCES

As a manager, you will have many resources to manage: people, budget, equipment, time, etc. For this chapter, your focus will be on your greatest and potentially (if not managed correctly) your most draining resource – you.

You: your **attitude**, your **behaviour** and your **skillset** to deliver the outcomes. These are the three key components to the Step-up Mindset.

Your attitude is the want to do something to the best of your ability. Your behaviour is the physical act of carrying out the tasks and activities, and your outcome is the reward for the right attitude and behaviour. Your resources may consist of equipment, people, budget, time, and more. The need to manage these effectively will create the environment for success.

Having the right toolkit to manage others and yourself effectively is a great starting point. Mentoring and coaching builds on this, and then having the freedom and support to learn (through your successes and errors) on the job is the ultimate support. Follow by paying this forward to the individuals within your team.

CHOICES

Everyone has choices. You may not perceive your choices as great or positive, but there are choices, and you will be required to choose.

You inevitably choose your outcomes by allowing your past experiences to influence your mood, and in turn attitude, behaviour and outcomes. Your attitude has been formed over time from your perceived experiences, your frame of reference. The word 'perceived' can be a hot button, as some regard perceived experience as real experience. And for you it is, but there are other people who may have been through the exact same experience and have perceived it differently, and so responded differently.

Your experiences mould you: they can define your thoughts and attitude. Think of a time when you were in a meeting, and afterwards you discuss what was said and covered within the meeting with your colleagues. As the conversation progresses you wonder, "Was I even in the same meeting?"; "I don't remember that"; "I thought this was what the meeting was about". It is not that your colleagues are lying about their experiences, or that you are lying; what you, and everyone else, are doing (regardless of age, gender, religion, etc.) is filtering the information to suit your frame of reference, your take on the world. It will be generalised, distorted and deleted at a subconscious level.

Generalise

There *is* a need to generalise information to ensure that it makes sense and can be quickly digested. What do you think when you see a group of teenagers? What are your immediate thoughts about the teenagers? What do you think when you see someone driving around in a Rolls Royce? What are you thinking about when you consider your future interactions with your manager? You are probably generalising based on your previous experience.

Distort

You will distort communications and information to your way of thinking to make sense of them. This might be a case of simplifying the communication, changing its context or rewording it.

Delete

When things don't make sense to you, you don't like what you hear or you don't have a vested interest in it, you delete the information. The key is knowing everyone around you is doing the same thing, and this is where communication often falls down. You as a manager must recognise this is happening and ensure that the message you are sending out is the same as the one being received.

You will look at this in more detail in a later chapter.

Your perception, your reality, your truth
Their perception, their reality, their truth

With the awareness that your experiences generally dictate your attitude, you realise attitude is learnt, and therefore it can be unlearnt and replaced (if need be) with something more rewarding. You have choices, and one of those is how you view life in general.

Positive mindset vs negative mindset

Take a moment to think of someone who is always negative.

- Is this person in your team?

- Is this person easy to manage?

- How much management time is spent with this individual?

Imagine for a moment that this person is on your team and you are to give them the great news they have a significant salary rise. What do you think will be their response?

I know from managing pessimistic and negative people what their answers will be:

"Guess you want blood for that."

"I expect you want me to work longer hours."

"I thought it would be more"

Are you Negative Nigel or Negative Nancy?

Attitudes are chosen and so can be changed. By reading this book, you have made it clear that you are looking to make changes and choose success. Use this book to create a more positive attitude, and align your attitude with your goals and outcomes.

Now, take a moment to think of someone who is always positive.

- Is this person in your team?

- Is this person easy to manage?

- How much of your management time is spent with this individual?

Imagine for a moment that this person is on your team and you are to give them the great news they have a significant salary rise. What do you think will be their response?

I know from managing optimistic and positive people what their answers will be:

"Woop-woop, yay."

"Wow, not sure I deserve this."

"Thank you for this, I will not let you down."

Are you Positive Patricia or Positive Peter?

Between the negative and positive mindset, whom would you rather work for? Who would get the best out of you? Who would create an environment for productivity? Whom would you rather have work with you? Who would get the best out of you and themselves? Who would help support an environment for productivity and promotion?

Having a positive Step-Up Mindset will make your journey so much more enjoyable and (dare I say it?) fun. Your attitude will help determine your success, although attitude alone will not work. You *must* follow through with behaviour.

With a positive attitude you will be able to recognise obstacles as challenges rather than allowing them to be the finishing line. You can look beyond what may be in your way and see your possibilities.

Of course, you can be overly positive and optimistic, and this leads to problems. Having an extremely optimistic view means that you may ignore issues and real concerns. Your outlook, whilst positive, may not be realistic. There is always balance, and realism must be included within an optimistic mindset. You will make the odd wrong decision, choose the wrong person, carry out the wrong task: that is called 'being human'.

Getting it wrong

To FAIL is the First Attempt In Learning. Life is a learning curve, and you will learn most from your mistakes. The Step-Up Mindset drives you forward, taking all the pleasure and pain and dealing with it.

The real world can be scary and exciting; it can be rushed and boring; it can be hard and soft; fun and hard work. With the Step-Up Mindset, you will see these are all partners:

parts of your journey. Acknowledging that some things will work and others will not (and are therefore learning opportunities) will carry you through the disappointment.

When you are in the Step-Up Mindset you will be prepared for many areas of success and some areas of disappointment. It will change how you view both your personal and professional life. Learning from mistakes and demonstrating those learnings will give you a sense of accomplishment.

One way of carrying this out is to prove you will not repeat the same mistake. Another is to implement processes to ensure the same mistake doesn't happen again, and there are many additional ways.

Energy and momentum

Energy levels are managed through positive thought, healthy eating and exercise. Within all three choices you have options either to build your energy or deplete it. To manage successfully you will need energy. On occasions, you will need energy to sustain others. Your team may be lacking motivation, and if you need to manage this, energy helps. Your manager may be off for a period of time and the expectation may fall to you to manage in their absence, so you will need energy.

As you start out in your management career, find positive energy boosters. Not synthetic ones, e.g. energy drinks, caffeine or other substances, but what motivates you. A little stress can be a great motivator, but a lot of stress is an energy and health stealer.

One of a manager's most supportive resources is their engagement with a mentor or coach. A great coach's support will help you achieve your goals. When your energy flags, your coach will work with you to find ways of boosting it naturally. Together you will explore what you are doing and why this is not motivating you, and assess whether there needs to be a re-steer, change of direction or even a complete overhaul of your goals. A coach will help you re-balance your workload, assist you in clearing out the unwanted and non-important noise and distractions, and ensure your challenges do not faze you. They inspire you. In fact, they energise you.

Sustaining your energy, productivity and motivation will often lead to further career opportunities.

Career progression

With the right mindset, you see career opportunities and have wishes. You will seize these opportunities and turn your wishes into reality. You will have a clear understanding of *why* you are working towards your goals, which will be your impetus and drive you forward, generating the behaviour that feeds your success. As you demonstrate your potential for your next role and every role after that, your reputation as a great manager will exceed you.

You have choices. Remember choosing wisely and getting it wrong is better than not making choices and playing it safe.

CHAPTER REFLECTION AND ACTION – THE STEP-UP MINDSET

Adopting the Step-Up Mindset is a choice. You can choose to continue as you are, or you can choose to change.

The Step-Up Mindset asks you to be aware of your environment and how you choose to react to it.

- Are you able to clearly identify your available resources, or is it you can only focus on the lack of resources?

- Can you recognise how you are distorting, generalising and deleting your thoughts and perceptions to make situations and scenarios more comfortable?

- Is your comfort zone in the negative or positive arena?

- Can you recognise this in others?

Now is the time to reflect. Highlight three situations from the last week and reflect on how they felt and how you reacted.

Remember: even carrying out this exercise you are distorting, generalising and deleting.

CHAPTER 3

FOCUS ON THE WHY

A CLEAR FOCUS ON THE WHY

If you know why you are working towards something, what your outcomes will be, how this fits into the bigger picture and it is compelling, you will have greater success. The alternative is working blind with no personal or emotional buy-in to the outcome. In other words, if you have clear sight of your 'why', you will have clear sight of your goal and the motivation to work towards your success.

Working towards any goal, objective, want or wish requires focus on the why. This will be the drive if things get tough or you are steered off track.

Finding your why

If you were to ask people around you why they work, the chances are their initial reaction will be "for the money". For most, though, this is not really the case. Money is important, it is just not the most important driver.

The driver is often something more inspiring: career change, career progression, personal challenge, learning experience. Find your own why. Simon Sinek, author of a great book on the subject *Start with the Why*, writes about the need to know your why before your what and how, and this is true in all your actions. If you do not know your why, you lose impetus, energy and direction.

Once you have a clear understanding of your why, then you will find your what and how. Knowing this will map out the behaviours required to deliver. You will review this in more detail as you go through the book.

The good, the bad and the downright ugly management engagement

In my varied career I have worked with many managers whose engagement styles can usually be categorised under the good, the bad or the downright ugly.

The good

When you think of a good manager, you may very well be thinking of someone who is a great communicator, gets the job done, whose team is happy and motivated, and I am sure there is a lot more besides.

I suspect that they took time to get to a place where they are admired and respected as a manager by others. Even for the best managers, it takes time to build up trust and respect from their team, colleagues and clients, and of course their own manager. It's not something that happens overnight, and nor should it be.

The good manager will have had a clear of understanding of *why* they are carrying out this role. There will be a personal and emotional connection for them to buy into.

The bad

When you think of a bad manager, you may well be thinking of someone who is just bad at what they do. They are probably a good person in the wrong job, or a good person who desperately requires development within their role. As time goes on for this individual and they get more things wrong than right, their confidence takes a nosedive. They may then lose the motivation to get the job right and take the easy option: bad communication, if any at all; lacklustre energy to get the job completed; a lacklustre team mirroring their manager, and lots more besides.

I suspect (and hope) they may have wanted to be good at their role when starting out, but it all became too difficult. They did not have a clear understanding of their why, and therefore no real concept of their what and how.

The downright ugly

When you think of an ugly (and I don't mean physically) manager, you may think of someone who is downright nasty; a deliberate and intentional act of bad management; someone who simply does not care. They know their why, but don't care about the what or how; they do not take into account anyone else, and they have no intention of changing. Their focus is purely on them and their needs and this may involve the task in hand. Without a strong mentor or coach, this manager will never change.

You have choices. How would you like to be seen? What will your team, manager, peers and clients say about you?

CHAPTER REFLECTION AND ACTION – DEFINING YOUR WHY

Consider the compelling reasons *why* you want to be a great manager. Your whys will change over time and your list of reasons will grow.

List your whys. Listed below are six possible whys to get you started:

1. career progression

2. love of the role

3. reputation

4. job satisfaction

5. learning

6. financial reward

CHAPTER 4

FOCUS ON YOUR
WHAT AND HOW

Team, task and self

As a new manager, and even more importantly when you are starting to develop yourself within the role, it is often easier if you are able to categorise your role and responsibilities.

One of the aims of this book is to take the mystery out of management, and to deliver this in a simple format. To meet this aim of simplicity, there are three key focus areas that you need to consider: self, team and task.

Self

It is impossible to manage an effective and efficient team if the manager takes no time to develop themselves. It is imperative as a manager that you understand who you are and where you are you going. Equally important is that you understand how you're going to get there, and how you are going to bring the team along with you.

Therefore one of the first areas you must consider is yourself. Get your stall in order as you start to work with your team, your clients, your colleagues and of course your manager.

Moving forward

In order to move forward, you must reflect on the past, have clear goals to work towards, and understand where you are today and where you want to be. Until you have clarity on where you are and where you want to be, it is impossible to gauge how to bridge the gap between the two places.

One goal you will hope to achieve by looking at these areas is to grow your confidence. Considering how you manage yourself alongside how you are going to manage your team and tasks will highlight areas for development, and also areas of strength.

Alice came to a fork in the road.

"Which road do I take?" she asked.

"Where do you want to go?" responded the Cheshire Cat.

"I don't know" Alice answered.

"Then," said the Cat, "it doesn't matter."

Lewis Carroll – Alice in Wonderland.

You do know where you want to go, therefore it does matter.

Your team can make or break your reputation

Your reputation as a manager is not solely judged on you. Do not kid yourself. Your reputation will be built up and tarnished by your team. Whilst you are responsible for your own reputation, your team's performance will also enhance or detract from it.

I have never met a great manager with a long-term awful team. However, I have met an awful manager with an awful team made up of great people. That in itself should tell you that teams are judged on their manager's skills and capability. Interestingly, a team that is delivering can still be seen as having a bad manager. A team that is underperforming will *always* be seen as having a bad manager.

Build confidence

One of the first areas to consider is how to build your confidence, followed by how to build others' confidence in you. Alongside this, how do you demonstrate that you are professional within your role? In order to do that you must consider your strengths and how you are going to utilise them, and you also want to challenge your weaknesses.

When you feel and demonstrate confidence, you will feel more in control. You'll know what you're doing; you will demonstrate to others that you are the right person for the job; and, of course, you will not suffer from 'impostor syndrome'.

By carrying this out, you demonstrate confidently that you can handle business in the good times as well as when it is not going so well. You will show others that you have a vision for the team, the service, and you will work with your clients to relate that vision back to their requirements. In order to show that you are a professional, you will have a plan in place of where you're going and a great understanding of where you are. You will set and communicate expectations for your team, your clients, your manager and peers.

Confidence is also demonstrated through taking a flexible approach. As things change and flex, you change and flex with them.

Another way of feeling and demonstrating confidence is by communicating the correct information to the relevant people. Information is disseminated in the right order and the right format, so very importantly, you need to use the right language.

Weaknesses and strengths

As a manager you will have a balanced view not only of yourself, your team and those around you, but also of your own strengths and weaknesses. Good managers challenge their obvious and not so obvious weaknesses as well as recognising and acknowledging their strengths. Taking time to reflect on this, you will recognise your strengths and you'll be able to put them into immediate use. You can look for quick wins to show you're the right person for the job, using those strengths in service where and when required.

When you challenge your weaknesses, you'll show the team that weakness is acceptable. It is something to be open with and supported. In order to have a balanced approach to your own weaknesses, you will find that sourcing feedback from others will give you a more realistic take on it.

Recognising your weaknesses will also give you the insight to consider others within the team, their strengths and capabilities. Is there someone within your team who is better at something than you are? If that is the case, do you want to utilise them for a particular task, or do you wish to improve your weak points? You will find if you recognise and acknowledge weaknesses as well as strengths within yourself and others, you will have more patience and clarity when dealing with them. You will understand whether weaknesses need to be supported. Do you or others need to be developed in that area, or is it an area that, put quite simply, will not impact the individual, their role or the business?

By taking the time to read this book and work through the 'Reflection and Action' chapters, you will already have begun the transition into the Step-Up Mindset.

MANAGEMENT STYLES

Googling management styles, you will discover hundreds and thousands of different styles. So many to remember, and so many to forget. As you are likely to be starting out within your management career while you read this book, it is important that you don't get hung up on the labels. Focus your attention more on the doing rather than what it is called.

I am going to cut through all the different labels and give you four simple styles to consider:

1. People Manager

2. Task Manager

3. Optimal Manager

4. Disengaged Manager

You will have a natural style you prefer to work within: a style that you do not think about. There will be other styles that bring you outside of your comfort zone and will need to be thought through in order to find your comfort zone and carry them out successfully.

Focus on three of the four styles: people, task, and optimal. Your aim should never be to work within the disengaged manager style. As a new or young manager, you may find it difficult to recognise the styles. You may also find it uncomfortable to adapt your mindset between the three styles, and this is perfectly normal. For now the focus is on when and where to use the different styles. Which style will work best for which scenario?

The best way to carry this out is through reflection. Be realistic with this: you will get it wrong at times, but the errors will decrease as time goes on. Remember it is less of a mistake if you can take and implement the learnings from the wrong choices.

Let's look at the styles in more detail.

PEOPLE MANAGER

For the most part this is an emotionally rewarding style to work within, the idea being that your team comes before everything else. You ensure that your team is well taken care of. You fight their every battle, aim to ensure they are happy at all times, but this can often be to the detriment of providing a great product or service to your clients.

The people manager is very nurturing and ensures the staff get the best of everything, including development, salary reviews and recognition. There are many advantages and disadvantages to this.

Advantages:

- staff feel very supported;

- staff feel they play an important part within the team;

- staff have confidence to be more creative and innovative within the rules;

- an environment is created whereby calculated risk is learnt from;

- there is a general sense of well-being within the department;

- work-life is proportionally balanced;

- the manager receives a high level of loyalty;

- when required, the team will often put extra hours in and go the extra mile to get a job completed, knowing that they will be recognised for their hard work;

- the team often works well together with no need for competition as everyone is recognised and supported.

The above are just some of the advantages of being a good people manager and believing in and supporting your team wholeheartedly. However, there is the other side of the coin. When you take the people management support to the extreme, there can be disadvantages and seriously negative outcomes.

Disadvantages:

- Staff become complacent due to the lack of responsibility and ownership required in their role – manager supports their staff regardless.

- Staff lose their confidence due to the manager assisting or even doing everything for them, or worse, the manager does it all without sharing the load.

- The manager feels emotionally and physically drained due to the amount of support they need to give.

- The team doesn't calculate risk appropriately due to the lack of ownership within their roles.

- Creativity and innovation are not regarded as important features for the individual staff – they very much depend upon the manager to deliver instruction and the way forward.

- Staff do not receive balanced constructive feedback reports.

- Staff have an unbalanced view of their own accomplishments, either believing that they are very good at something when they are not, or believing that they're not good at something when they are. This is due to only ever receiving positive feedback and no constructive feedback to learn from.

One of my first roles in training, I worked for an exceptionally nice manager. In the 12 months that I worked with him I never once witnessed him get annoyed or raise his voice. He was calm and always supportive – sometimes too supportive.

Initially, it was wonderful working with him. He ensured that his team (there were four trainers) had everything that we required. When his trainers (including myself) had a reasonably long week of training and travelling, it was not unusual to come into the office and find our training materials and admin prepared in advance by the manager. It was also not unusual to come into the office when we were having a calmer week and find that he had still prepared a lot of our admin and materials.

This was great for the trainers until we started to expect it, and he didn't always have the time to deliver. In addition to this, he was forever telling us, and others, how great his team was; how we always delivered; how the feedback we received was fantastic. On the few occasions that he did receive negative feedback, without asking for the trainers' input he would refute the claim and tell the trainer not to worry. Initially this was reassuring, but before long I became unsure whether I was genuinely doing a good job, an okay job or even a bad job as the feedback from my manager was always amazingly positive. For me there was no learning from that role.

The people manager held one-to-one meetings as well as team meetings on a weekly basis. These meetings always ended up being social gatherings with no real direction other than "keep up the great job". In addition, we (the trainers) always seemed to be in his office spending much of our time talking about life and the universe, which did on occasions feel like I was wasting my time and effort when there was so much more I could bring to the role.

You will not please everyone all the time, so don't try. It will only lead to pleasing no one any of the time. When you displease someone, it is great feedback: it gives you a benchmark to improve upon. I was very grateful to have met my people manager and to have had such a nice boss; I was not so thankful to leave the role with no tangible new skills or challenging tasks to add to my CV.

TASK MANAGER

The task manager is such a different kettle of fish. Their main concerns (often only concerns) are the delivery and the outcomes; they are very much about delivering on what has been agreed, and may over-deliver on expected outcomes, giving additional value and greater impact to the customer. They drive the department forward with a clear understanding of how and what the team should be working towards, and the results of the outcomes are measurable. It's clear whether success has been reached, and success is often the case.

The task manager does not put much emphasis on the team's personal needs, e.g. development, workloads, etc., instead doing whatever is necessary to deliver on agreements. Therefore they work very well with service level agreements and time-bound outcomes and goals, but there is often no room for debate with the task manager. They are too focused on the need to deliver, and in their opinion they know best how to carry this out.

As with any management style, there are always pros and cons.

Advantages:

- there is an expectation from customers to have their requirements met each and every time, proven through constant delivery;

- measurable success and clear outcomes;

- process-driven tasks;

- everyone understands the goals;

- staff know what is expected of them.

The above are just some of the advantages. There are also disadvantages.

Disadvantages:

- tasks can be prioritised over the welfare of the staff;

- unrealistic deadlines may be set;

- there is no room for negotiation: task delivery is the ultimate goal;

- manager can take on more than can be physically delivered, therefore placing pressure on the team;

- the manager may be measuring success based purely on task delivery;

- the team has no personal development;

- no loyalty from either staff or manager.

The job that I took on following working for the people manager was to work directly for a task manager. This was a real shock to the system. Having come from a role where I had been supported and nurtured and closeted from any negative influences, I walked into a role where I was held responsible for everything, including external forces I had no control over.

The task manager I was working for (and I use the phrase 'working for' rather than 'working with' deliberately as at no point did I feel part of his team or receive any support from him) had only one goal: to deliver on time and without being seen to have failed in any of the process. It was all about the task and not about the people.

This manager's style was to get things done regardless of external influences or forces, often with his team begrudgingly working late into the evening, coming in early and missing lunch and breaks. He applied pressure not only to myself, but to everyone, and his team had to deliver exactly what was asked and on time. If they didn't, there was no opportunity to give reasons for this. He would always assume the worst with regards to the team members' capabilities and skill sets, delivering this feedback in a punishment format that involved shouting and criticism. However, when things went well, he never gave any recognition for a good job completed. Where there were skillset deficiencies, they were never recognised and therefore never addressed. Overall, he had a general lack of interest in staff welfare or progression.

OPTIMAL MANAGER

The optimal manager is the best of the four styles to work within as they take a 360° approach to their team and tasks. The optimal manager will be aware of the necessity to be flexible and work with confidence through concerns and issues without sabotaging either the task or support for their team. This comes with experience: it can't be bought or borrowed.

There is always going to be a need to be flexible and on occasion work between the task manager, people manager and optimal manager styles. There is never a need or requirement to adopt the disengaged manager approach, unless, of course, you want to fail at your role.

You may well want to put on your task manager hat when there is no room for negotiation and the task is to be carried out within an impending deadline; when you are delivering a piece of legislation, a new process, Health and Safety procedures and want complete compliance from the team; when there is a crisis, possibly a last minute request. You will be required to deliver instruction assertively with no room for compromise or debate at the point of instruction.

The fundamental difference will be once the crisis is over and you have time to breathe, you will put your optimal manager hat back on and deliver to the team involved the reasons behind the need to follow the instruction as tasked without the usual collaborative take. By explaining these reasons, you will build trust and respect from your team. They will know that when your back is against the wall and there is no time for niceties, you will follow up with a meeting to communicate the reasons behind the urgency.

You will also need at times to be the people manager, for example when there is a genuine need for the team or individuals within the team to receive additional support, development, coaching or mentoring, or even just a need to feedback and listen to your team. The people manager hat should be placed on when you're in team meetings, one-to-ones, with new starters, introducing new processes that will have a major impact on individuals and at appraisal time. As I said in an earlier chapter, when you are required to wear this hat you need to wear it authentically and honestly. The focus must remain with the individual and not on the task when wearing the people manager hat.

DISENGAGED MANAGER

Oh, what a treat this manager is to work for. The disengaged manager cares about nothing and no one. They like to delegate full responsibility as well as tasks, and do not care about the tasks or their team. The disengaged manager is possibly a great game player, but not an honest or authentic manager, and certainly not likeable.

This is not a style to which you ever aspire.

Being able to balance out when each of the other three management styles is required will give you a greater level of confidence and success. Balance is fundamental to any role, regardless of seniority.

LAW OF BALANCE

Before going any further, you need to be clear, and I mean *very* clear, on the Law of Balance.

You must understand that balance is not necessarily a line in the middle of a page. For some, balance may be 75% work and 25% personal life. For others it may be the opposite, or anything in between. Without a doubt, whatever your balance is, you need to be very aware of how it works: it is all about give and take.

The Law of Balance always comes into play. If you take something, e.g. time off work, time away from family and friends, additional responsibility, you give something up. Taking time off work may result in giving up some salary. Time away from family and friends gives you extra time elsewhere. Additional responsibility means you are more than likely going to lose time for carrying out your current responsibilities.

Having a clear idea of how the Law of Balance works and then applying it to your work and personal life will give you greater understanding of your why (or maybe why not), and this will help you to meet your goal. When you say no to something, you will get balance with a yes to something else. When you say no to working late, you are saying yes to more personal time. When you say no to working full-time and potential additional salary, you are saying yes to more time for other areas of your life. When you take on additional team members, then you have to give something up, and this may be the amount of time spent with current team members or on particular tasks. If you were to take this further you'll possibly see a need to delegate certain tasks, and delegating them will bring you extra time. Or possibly you may choose to spend more time at work.

Think about the management styles. When you put on the task manager hat, you are primarily focusing your attention on tasks and outcomes, and therefore you are giving up focusing quite as much time on the people side of your role. This is also true when you put on your people manager hat. Your primary focus is on the people, and therefore there is less focus on the tasks and outcomes.

Aligning your focus and knowing your goal must be your top business priority, as well as having a very clear understanding on how to motivate your team and make the best of your other resources to achieve that. The optimal management style will give you the most satisfaction and will show others that you have the correct mindset to consider all aspects of management, not just getting the job done or thinking about the team. An added bonus is that you will get respect from within your team and your internal and external customers. When talking with your customers you will have the foresight to think of the big picture, and this will allow you to schedule outcomes better as you will consider the workloads of your staff and all additional resources required, e.g. budgets, stock, time, etc. Therefore you will be setting everybody, including yourself, up for success.

If you were only to consider your staff (people manager), your deadlines would be so far in the future that they would not meet your customers' requirements, and the customers would be less than thrilled with the long times to delivery. If you were only to consider the task (task manager), you would be promising your customers everything, and eventually your team would get tired of the undue stress and leave, in turn creating delivery issues.

The advantages of being within an optimal manager mindset very much speak for themselves: you have more balance, you're more logical in your approach, and it becomes a natural progression to move from people manager to task manager or remain within optimal manager mode as required. This is a definite requirement of a great manager.

CHAPTER REFLECTION AND ACTION – MANAGEMENT STYLES

Within this book, there are four very simple management styles to recognise, and three (people, task and optimal) that you will develop.

You will have a natural and preferred style. The aim of this chapter is to recognise your preferred style and adjust your attitude and behaviour to be fluent in moving between people, task and optimal manager. Disengaged manager is not an option.

Answer the following:

When have you observed each of the management styles in others?

- Which style received the best reception?

- Consider your everyday work scenarios, allocate the best management style to these.

- Which of the three styles feels easier, more comfortable for you?

This is now the time to sit back and reflect on your strengths and your weaker styles. There is an absolute need for each of the three management styles within your role. It is your responsibility to be aware of and consider what different scenarios will occur, and where you might use the different management styles.

Calendar in daily reflection time

I would also add, and actively encourage, that at the end of each day or week you take time to reflect on the scenarios and measure whether you believe that you carried out the communication correctly with the correct management style.

CHAPTER 5

ATTITUDE – FIRST COMPONENT TO THE STEP-UP MINDSET

FLIGHT, FIGHT OR FREEZE

Your (and everyone else's) attitudes are formed directly from your frame of reference, based on perceived past experiences. (You briefly read about this in Chapter 2. Remember, you have choices. You choose a productive or non-productive attitude.)

Attitudes can be driven by fear. When you are fearful, you respond with fight, flight or freeze. When you start to own and choose your journey, you may well set goals so great and possibly so challenging that you start to question yourself. Am I capable? Do I have the time? Is it worth it?

You can choose fight, flight or freeze, or even to change the goal. Flight is the easy option: you decide not to continue with the goal and walk (or run) away from it. Fight is facing your fear and doing it anyway. Freeze is to continue to persecute yourself with "I should be doing this" and staring at it with no action.

I often think in this case freeze is a worse mindset than flight. At least with flight, you want to forget all about it. With freeze you continuously look at your goals without acting, which is the most toxic option of the three.

Flight

If your natural tendency is flight, then stop and ask: "Why is this my natural option? Is my motivation clear? Do I understand my why? Have I calculated the balance of this goal? Do I understand what this goal will give me? Is this goal compelling enough to drive me past my fear and take action?"

The next time you are faced with the want to fly, take some time out and review your goal and your why. Ask yourself, "What do I need to do to make me really want to meet this goal?"

You may have worded the goal as a negative, e.g. "I don't want to be doing this job in 6 months", or you may have worded it in a fluffy context, "I want another job". Neither of these are clear goals, so you need to reword the goal to make it more compelling; more rewarding; more a hunger than a maybe.

You will find the chapter on TRUST explains this in more detail, and this will assist you in getting clarity around your goal.

Fight

Now this is the mindset that screams, "I am stepping up to a manager's mindset." You see your goal as a challenge. You know your why, you understand what is in it for you, you see the big picture and you go for it. You step off the cliff, knowing there is a net there to catch you.

Freeze

Ah, the freeze mode: the one that hurts your productivity, confidence and mindset the most. This is the one that you use to beat yourself up with. You know the goal might help you, and the 'might help' is stronger than the motivation to fly from it, but not strong enough to fight for it. This is the 'sitting on the fence' and not having the confidence to jump.

If this is your natural choice, then stop. Just stop and breathe. You need a clearer idea of your why and what is in it for you. You must make the goal compelling enough and then choose to carry it out.

"Get off the fence, you wuss!" is what I would like to shout, I am just way too professional to do that.

What will your attitude do for you?

It will do whatever you choose. If you choose a negative attitude, it will ensure that you are proven right. All the things that happen to you, around you and inside your frame of reference will feed your negative attitude. It will allow you to see only the bad, the negative, the unjust, and they will feed the 'if it is going to happen, it will happen to me' victim approach. Your attitude will ensure that everything is hard work.

Negative attitudes do not make life easy. If life was easy you would not have the opportunity to play the victim.

Your attitude gives you choices

If you choose a positive attitude, it will ensure that you are proven right. All the things that happen to you, around you and inside your frame of reference will feed your positive attitude. When you come across challenging situations, you will manage them better, using your energy to resolve rather than moan.

Remember, you need balance in life. If you don't have the challenges, you will never know your potential. You need the negative to realise the positive; balancing how you handle the situations is key to your success. Allowing negativity to be your attitude is your key to hardship and victimisation.

Your attitude alone will not determine your success; there is also a need to follow through with behaviour. However, without the right attitude, success will elude you. Attitude will be a key definer in your reputation and brand. You own your attitude; it is your responsibility to ensure that it is a well-oiled machine cared for and serviced on a regular basis, which involves engaging in formal MOTs, and the MOTs must be carried out more frequently than annually. In fact a weekly or even daily MOT is often required.

Is my attitude fit for purpose? Does it drive me in the direction I want to go in? Does it build my brand and reputation? If the answer to the questions is no, your attitude needs some work, but do not lose heart. Remember attitudes are learnt and therefore can be unlearnt. Unproductive and negative attitudes can be swapped for more productive and positive attitudes.

If your answer to the questions is yes, great. In both cases, keep reading as you are about to drive your success forward.

Align your attitude to your role

Aligning your attitude to your role will assist you in recognising when your attitude needs to be adjusted for different scenarios and situations. You may know from experience that a person's attitude is often the one thing that others will talk about.

You may have heard: "He has the skills to carry out the job, he just doesn't have the attitude" or "I think that she is capable of the job, but her attitude stinks" or "He doesn't have the skills for the role, but he does have the right attitude. You can develop skill sets within individuals, but it is more difficult to realign someone's attitude".

The last statement is an interesting one. As you progress through life and your career, you will be required to realign your attitude to your role.

Attitude and authority

Your attitude demonstrates your level of authority. If you are not assertive within your role and you say yes to everyone and everything, you will find that you don't deliver anything to anyone. People will consider that you are a junior within the team.

"Why is this?" I hear you ask. This is because people expect a manager or team leader to have a better understanding of the services and products they provide than a junior team member. A manger should be aware of (or at least be analysing) the resources that are required to deliver their offerings before agreeing to the delivery. Never set yourself, or others, up for failure.

Take control

It is important that you align your attitude to stepping up and taking control. By using the word control, I certainly don't mean that you micromanage everything. I use the word control this way to mean managing your team and outputs and outcomes.

You are the decision maker

It is important as a new manager that you take responsibility and make decisions. You must use your own initiative, add to this well thought-through logic and a good attitude, and you will have a greater understanding of the task in hand.

At the beginning of this chapter you read that your attitude is based on your frame of reference. Therefore if you are someone who generally shies away from making decisions, now is the time to breathe and put your best foot forward. This may feel alien to you, but it is a must in any management role, regardless of whether you are a junior or on your way through to the Chief Executive's position.

One way to do this is to review all the options available to you, and this can be achieved through working with your team (remember, there may be a better person for the task in hand than yourself), working with tools, methodologies and other available resources. (You will read more on tools and methodologies at a later stage in the book.)

One of the most recurring concerns I hear from my clients, particularly those who have recently been internally promoted, is how they want to make their mark in the role, but they don't have time. In order to have the bandwidth to make decisions and carry out their role at the appropriate level, they must make the time, but when I work with them and explore how they spend their time, there is a recurring trend: they want to retain their old responsibilities. The new manager is either unsure of how to delegate, or more often than not, they simply want to keep what they do well to themselves.

This manager needs to have a Step-Up Mindset in place, which will ensure that they are confident enough to hand over some, or maybe even all, of their previous role's tasks. They need to feel in control enough to know that the final outcome will be as they would have wished.

When that is not the case, the manager's role becomes a bottleneck. They will stop production from happening as they still carry out their previous job whilst trying to take on the new job. It's important that new managers (any managers, in fact) delegate. (There is more on this later in the book.) If they do not delegate their previous role's tasks and responsibilities, they will do neither their new nor previous role successfully.

Remember the Law of Balance? Ensure you plan and execute a programme that gives you confidence to hand over previous tasks, and that includes the what, to whom, and when. And, of course, some thought to the what is in it for the delegate?

Mate to manager

If you have been working within your team and have been promoted internally to team leader or manager, in some (not all) circumstances this can cause issues. If you take into account this may be a sensitive point for some and think through how to motivate your team, you are on the right track. Know, though, in real life, no matter how considerate you are, the team will find something to moan about with their colleagues, and often that something is you.

I suspect at some point within your more junior role you have probably complained about your manager, processes, the company, and everything else in between. As the manager, you are now the one the team will be complaining about. This is normal, accept it, and get on with the job.

Taking the good with the bad

One of the most liberating moments of my career came when I adjusted my attitude. I made the conscious decision to take ownership and responsibility not just for the team, but also for the inputs and outcomes. I sat back and reflected on what managers' responsibilities are, not just their physical tasks and outputs, and took time to consider the emotional impact of this decision. I would not always get what I wanted, feedback would be sparse, I would get things wrong, and not always hear about what I got right. I would be unsure of myself, sometimes it would feel as if I had bitten off more than I could chew, etc.

One emotional impact was to take responsibility when things went wrong and praise when things went right. At the time I was working for a manager who was very much siding with the blame culture. He would ensure anything that was not carried out to his standard would be highlighted as an enormous mistake (even though it was often a minor error), and the blame would then be assigned to an individual or individuals.

Initially, my response was to mirror that management style (100% task manager), and then project my unhappiness on to the team. I learnt very quickly that working within a blame culture stifles productivity, demotivates staff and is toxic to my attitude, behaviour and those around me, and I decided that I was going to turn things around and change my attitude.

One of my first acts was to take ownership and responsibility, and equally to support the team through the good and the bad. With these attitudes changed, I made the conscious decision that when my manager pointed the finger at me, my response would be positive. I would consider the best resolution to the problem rather than my initial response, which was to think whom I could blame. I also started to change the language I used with my team and internally. Instead of making excuses and using negative words and phrases, I chose to swap into positive responses. When I was blamed for something, I would not come back with a response that could be construed as an excuse. My response would be, "Let me look into this and get to the bottom of the issue".

Once I had carried this out (it was more often than not a communication issue rather than an operational issue), I would look for a resolution with the help of my team. I would then feed back to my manager and let him know the resolution (where applicable) and give him a brief (high-level, not detailed) overview of the cause of the issue, always highlighting the great input from the team.

My overall hope was that whilst I couldn't change my manager, possibly I could influence him. However, what I knew for sure was that I could change my own attitude. The outcome for me was that I was much more positive with work and recognised my manager's faults. As a result of my new-found attitude and follow-up behaviour, work became manageable and enjoyable.

I would highly recommend as you go through this book and apply the learnings back in the workplace that you consciously step-up and take ownership of the good and the bad. Change any negatives into positive thoughts and actions. One of the easiest ways to carry this out is to reflect on what went wrong and learn from it.

To take this a stage further, take actions to ensure that the learnings are put into place and the mistakes and errors are not repeated. That alone will make you more confident within your role and reinforce to yourself and your team that a positive mindset is more productive and rewarding than a negative one.

Promoted for potential, paid for performance

An issue that you may be experiencing, or you may be facing from your team, is inadequate reward for promotion.

If you have recently been promoted, I would hope it was based on both your performance to date and your potential within your new role. There may have been some form of reward assigned to you when you were promoted. If so, congratulations. If not, choose the positive route and prove you are the right person for the role. A great attitude, high performing behaviour and resulting successful outcomes will demonstrate this. You certainly have a better chance of being rewarded for delivering a great job than for the possibility you may carry out a great job, and at worst you will have a good attitude and invaluable experiences that will carry you through to your next role.

Remember, it is more and more common in the workplace to be promoted on potential and paid for performance. The only way of influencing the decision makers is to demonstrate your worth through delivery.

Pursuing promotion

If you are looking for promotion within your company, be aware of what needs to take place in order for you to be considered for the new role. Promotion is generally based on your potential, and the only way to show your potential is to stand out in your current role. That means taking on more responsibility (remember the Law of Balance), being more creative and getting yourself known for the right reasons. Be seen to be a team player, someone who is dependable and delivers, someone who networks well, someone who motivates their team, before stepping up to a new role and reaping the benefits.

You will frequently come across issues with members of staff who believe that they are not being paid enough, or believe that they should be paid for promotion. As their manager you need to have a frank and honest discussion with them whilst offering support to bring them to a place of demonstrating their performance. Set up timelines and targets, and get buy-in from the employee to work towards them. Do not set them up for failure – it will not only reflect badly on them, it will reflect badly on you – and ensure you only offer what you are able to deliver to the employee. Do not promise £x after their probationary period if you have not received the confirmation prior to the meeting. Make sure any agreements are in writing (even in an email), and all parties involved, your manager, HR, Finance, etc., are in the loop.

If you are the one who feels put upon, apply the same logic with your manager. Agree timelines, progress checks and, ideally, rewards. Always remember the other side of the coin: when you get promoted, you must perform at the new more senior level. If you are delivering at a junior level whilst being paid at a more senior level, this is damaging to all concerned and often leads to the manager questioning their decision to promote you.

CHAPTER REFLECTION AND ACTION – ALIGN YOUR ATTITUDE

Your attitude is a crucial component within your success or failure.

There will be times when your attitude aligns perfectly with your role, and other times when it does not. As a manager, it is your responsibility to choose what will motivate you into aligning your attitude with your role.

Answer the following questions, being honest with yourself:

- What situations have you experienced that you responded to with:

    o flight?

    o freeze?

    o fight?

- What was it that instigated the response?

- Was the outcome of the responses positive or negative?

- What could you do differently next time if you came across the same situation?

- How do you respond to criticism?

- How can you take a criticism and reframe it as a learning opportunity?

- What can/do you do to take note of the learnings?

- What is your process/can your process be for taking action from those learnings?

- When are you least happy with at work?

- What can you do to change this?

- What one thing (with regards to attitude) will you change that will make a difference?

CHAPTER 6

BEHAVIOUR –
SECOND COMPONENT
TO THE STEP-UP
MINDSET

Working over the years has given me great exposure to many roles, either through experience or observation. The one pattern of behaviour I have seen over and over again is a role with clear expectations delivering a different set of behaviours and outcomes. Examples include when a manager is still in the mindset of their previous role, or does everything themselves and does not delegate, or works alone and forgets about the team, or whose only concern is the tasks or people...I could go on, but I am hoping you're seeing where I am going.

Can you recognise any of these examples in others? What about yourself?

Having the right behaviour assists the delivery of the right outcomes

Having the right attitude without the behaviour is the same as having a great looking car without the engine. It will not drive you anywhere. You need the behaviour to execute your goals. You need the behaviour to choose fight over flight or freeze.

Can you think of someone who has the right attitude, always wants to help, says yes to most things, gets heavily involved and never delivers? Their reputation and brand is probably something along the lines of 'Great person, not dependable'. You begin to stop involving them in tasks and projects. You raise an eyebrow when their name is mentioned, for whilst you trust that they will be positive with their thinking (attitude), they will be horrendous with their delivery (behaviour).

Behaviour vs skillset

Behaviour and skillset are very different. A skillset can be defined as a collection of learnt skills, e.g. finance, HR, communication, time management, etc. Behaviour is physical demonstration, the 'doing'.

You read the earlier example of someone having a great attitude and never following up with actions, but the same can be said of someone having a lazy attitude yet getting things done. Imagine working with someone who has a negative mindset and attitude. They will probably carry out just enough work to get by, possibly whinging and moaning their way through all work related tasks, and this is an example of lousy attitude with some delivery.

Whom would you prefer to work with: great attitude and no follow through, or negative attitude and minimum delivery?

On many of my development workshops I've posed this same question, and 90% of the trainees answered that they would like to work with someone who had a great attitude but never delivered. Many managers feel that those individuals can be developed in order to have a great attitude and delivery.

What was your answer?

Behaviour is fundamental to success. It goes hand-in-hand with attitude and is very much complemented with skillset. All three need to be congruent in order to deliver.

Align your behaviour to your role

Just as you read in Chapter 5 about aligning your attitude to your role, the same is true of your behaviour.

You must be able to demonstrate your aptitude for the role. This has to be more than talking or thinking: there has to be action and outcomes, and these can only be achieved through doing.

It is crucial to ensure that your behaviour is befitting of your role. You must know what management behaviour would look like at your position and ensure that you use this as a benchmark (the benchmark being the minimum level of behaviour that you will be delivering). Remember, you get promoted on potential and paid on performance.

As a new manager you will be looking to demonstrate your behaviour to more people: customers, peers, your manager, as well as the business and external influences. It is important that you push yourself forward, striving for success. After all, there is no point in standing still – your role won't.

Your behaviour is tangible

Your behaviour, and everybody else's behaviour, can be measured. Therefore, it is a gauge of success or failure. Often, when something doesn't work, there will be extenuating circumstances, and as a manager you need to recognise whether attitude and behaviour are the success blockages, or are they external influences that cannot be managed? You need to recognise if it is your behaviour and its impact on your team that is cancelling out success, remembering the good, the bad and the downright ugly management engagement styles.

Any way you wrap this up, behaviour can and should be a measure for personal and team success. If it does not measure up, it must be addressed.

Quick wins

Quick wins are often a great way of showing your detractors (if you have any) that you're the right person for the role. Having an understanding of the problems faced by the department, the business and your clients will help you define quick wins over long-term wins and impact.

Later in the book you will read a chapter on carrying out task audits with your department, which may be the measurements that you work on to produce the wins for your customers, manager, peers, team and the business as a whole. For longer term wins and goals, you must demonstrate that you have an understanding (attitude) of issues and that you will be, or are, working (behaviour) on solutions. Behaviour is very much about being proactive within your role. Yes, reactive is a must, and it is better to be reactive than non-active, but in an ideal world you will be working 80% proactively and 20% reactively. Reality shows that managers tend to work 20% proactively and 80% reactively.

My challenge to you is to get closer to being proactive rather than reactive.

Be confident in your delivery

Be knowledgeable on why you are delivering a particular task in a particular manner. By you, I could mean your team or an individual within your team as well as you yourself. This knowledge comes with experience and time within the role. There is only so long that you can sit thinking about and exploring all aspects before action is required. You must be able to communicate why you chose your particular route and the outcomes, even if just to yourself. This will give you the confidence to get going and help you take constructive feedback graciously as a learning opportunity and not as a personal slight on your management skills.

Take constructive feedback graciously

To improve upon anything in life, you need to have a rounded approach to feedback, both the good and the constructive. You can of course improve upon things without external influences and feedback, but having them will help shape your decisions and confirm that you are working on the right areas.

As a new manager you will have to give feedback, and should be actively looking to garner feedback when it is not being offered. When feedback is positive it is very easy to be gracious. When feedback is constructive criticism, or worse delivered negatively, it can be somewhat more difficult to be gracious. However, as a manager you must take all feedback, including examples of when your attitude or outcome wasn't as expected, and look to learn from it.

You read earlier about managers I have coached, developed, and worked with who had been carrying out their role at a junior level. The impact of this was that they were not able to see the wood for the trees in their new role. They could not see what needed to be focused on, only what was going well in their old role.

Behaviour is all about demonstrating that you are carrying out your management role and having the greatest impact possible.

NETWORKING FOR SUCCESS

With your attitude and behaviour in positive alignment, you will want to start reaping the benefits of this. As a new manager you will ideally want to get your reputation and brand out there. It may be tempting to want, and indeed start building, a relationship with everybody you meet within your role, but practicalities may deem this impossible within the company (depending on its size).

You absolutely 100% want to build a strong support base around you through relationships and networking, but choose your networking wisely. If you make the time to nurture your networks, and therefore nurture the relationships formed within these networks, you may find that working together will be a much more collaborative experience, including more open, honest and productive relationships.

When forming a network, take spending the time on this into account within your goal. Networks are all about give and take, and that means you must consider the Law of

Balance. The time you give to networking must be taken from somewhere else. Where will that be?

Ensure that your contribution to the network is authentic. By authentic, I mean build a network that you are prepared to give to as much as take from. In fact, I would go as far as to write that authentic relationships are built more on how much you are prepared to give than receive.

Authentic networks

Authentic really is a genuine want to be supportive of others, so authentic networks are built on trust and respect from all parties involved. Within an authentic network, each person will intuitively know that they've got the support and trust of the other members. Trust is built through repetitive actions so it may take time for it to happen, but stick with it. It will be worth it.

I am sure you know someone you can trust each and every time to support you, and I'm sure you know someone who you can trust to get it wrong every time. You trust this because both of these individuals have proven it over and over again.

Building a great network

Choose existing networks, for example LinkedIn, internal forums, external associations, and build your own more informal networks.

Networks should involve many different types of individuals, not just those from your work or those who are in the same or a similar role type as yourself. They should include customers (where appropriate), your team, your manager as well as other colleagues internally and externally.

It is always an idea to include senior individuals too. In authentic and sincere networks, senior individuals will often act as informal mentors to those less experienced, and hopefully one day you will pay that forward. Networking is not an accounting system; not about tit-for-tat – I do one thing for you, then you do one thing for me. Authentic and sincere networks are about supporting each other and helping each other when needed.

When you have the opportunity to include customers within your network, this has great benefits for both you and them. Having the level of trust and respect that a good network generates between its members can be vital when push comes to shove. You will find that if you have a good relationship with your customers (regardless of whether you believe them to be part of your network or not), when you or your department makes the odd mistake (and you are only human), they will hopefully want to work in partnership with you to correct it rather than use it as a whipping point to get one up on you.

Great marketing opportunity

Networks that include both clients and internal staff give you the opportunity to create a great platform from which to market yourself, your department, your company and your successful outcomes.

I often hear, "I do not like marketing myself, it feels like I am being big–headed and I don't want to come across as arrogant". Arrogance only comes across when delivered in an arrogant manner. It is not arrogance to share your news, and marketing is a form of sharing. It's a way to inform others what you've completed and what you are planning on doing, and hear what others have done – it is not one sided! Marketing is about sharing your and your department's offerings, letting others know what you can do for them and letting external contacts know the business's successes. It is not about selling your service or extending the truth.

Referrals

The best form of marketing is word-of-mouth, and the best form of word-of-mouth is referrals. In order for someone to refer you, your department or your company, they need to know what you are about. They will need to be reassured that you will not let them down. After all, if a referral turns bad it reflects badly on the referrer as well as the referred company.

In an ideal world, the referrer will have experienced first-hand your offering and will be able to talk about it with a sense of conviction. They will need to understand what your successes and outcomes look like, including within this the value add and positive impact. They must have the conviction that you are not only going to provide the referee with great services, but your offering will reflect well on them.

Therefore, see marketing as a way of extending your reputation and brand, and that of your department and company. What could be better than receiving new clients through referrals, and not having to do the work of the sales and marketing team?

Always remember to give others the opportunity to network and market themselves to you. You will then be able to refer them on, particularly if you have experienced their service and highly rate it. It feels great to refer someone. In a world where we are so quick to judge and voice negative comments about suppliers, it is a breath of fresh air when someone has something positive to say. What's more, when you do receive a referral you are more likely to engage with that company than go out and source suppliers from elsewhere.

Networking: quality vs quantity

If you do feel inclined to build a large network in order to market yourself, typically this will be carried out at an established networking event or speed networking. You will find you have a very short time to talk with everyone – after all, it is about quantity and not quality. Typically, you become one of a crowd, a faceless name. Or worse, a member of the group is interested in the service you offer, but cannot recall who they spoke to.

There is a very real danger of spreading yourself too thinly at these types of events. You may receive genuine interest in your product or service but not recognise it and therefore miss an opportunity to follow up. This is because the volume of people you have met has just become noise.

If you want to be a big fish in a small pond, if you want to be that go to person, ensure your impact is great. Is it not better to please a customer who comes back with repeat business than have to please lots of customers who come only once? If you have a client giving you repeat business, the chances are you will get a referral from them. You may have to ask, but that's not a bad thing!

If you dilute your impact by increasing your network, going for quantity over quality, then you may not be in a position to serve everyone and exceed their expectations each and every time. You may be offering your customers bland outcomes, only just producing what they asked for and expected rather than giving them outcomes that will delight and make them want to return. This of course is possibly what your competitors are offering too, but it doesn't allow you to stand out from the crowd, so why would they come back to you?

What would be worse? What if your competitors are offering a standout service and networking with a few rather than targeting a lot? They are receiving the repeat business, getting the referrals, keeping the select few exceptionally happy whilst you, with no real goal or outcome or measurement other than sales, are spreading yourself too thinly. It's highly likely you're spreading your team too thinly too and not thinking about the impact on your customer.

Critical and key relationships

As you consider who would be in your great support network (remember to give as well as take), there is a need to give great consideration to who are your critical and key relationships.

Critical relationships

Critical relationships are defined as those whom you depend upon to carry out your work, and those who depend upon you to carry out their work. If you consider yourself as part of the supply chain, who could not do their job without you? And whom could you or your team not do your job without?

Identifying your critical relationships will (ideally) help streamline the delivery process and reflect well on you and your team. Your critical relationships are absolutely fundamental to your success, and within the supply chain they are almost always internal individuals.

On occasions, as part of the big (business-wide) picture, you may have to sabotage your plans in order to gain overall success. The sabotage may involve putting your plans on the back-burner, or carrying out additional tasks that you may not perceive as being part of your team's role. This can be uncomfortable for you and your team, but it is vital that you understand what the big picture looks like, ensure that you play your part in it and are ready to support your critical relationships. Ensure that you are not working in silo or autonomously.

Key relationships

Key relationships are defined as those who assist in making your life easier. In the workplace they may be in ICT. If you have a high dependency (and in today's world, who does not?) on IT, you may wish to include the manager of ICT in your key relationship network. Do you rely on Finance to get invoices paid on time in order that you can place orders? Is Marketing the key to the smooth running of your department? Your key relationships will not have a direct impact on your offerings; what they will do is contribute to the smooth running of your department, and you can enhance this by ensuring that they are part of your network.

CHAPTER REFLECTION AND ACTION – IT IS ALL ABOUT YOU

When you think of a good manager, think about how they manage themselves as well as how they manage the other aspects of their role.

- What are the key attributes they demonstrate?

- What is it about their attitude that you admire?

- Which of the attributes do you currently demonstrate?

- What steps must you take to introduce new attributes?

- What can you do to enhance existing attributes?

Critical and key contacts

- Where does your department fit in within the supply chain?

- Whom are you dependent upon to get the job done?

- Who depends on you to carry out their role?

- Who, or what departments, will make your life easier in the workplace?

- Name three colleagues who are key contacts that you would like to strengthen your relationship with. What will you do to enable this?

CHAPTER 7
TEAM

Managing a team can be a full-time job in itself, and in the real world, as a manager you will have other roles and responsibilities to carry out as well as managing your team. In order to get the best from your team, you need to gain an understanding of what motivates them, how you build a greater team, and then maintain the team's motivation and productivity.

The key to a productive, motivated and efficient (take as far as self-sufficient) team is knowing them on an individual level: their strengths and weaknesses, what they like and do not like, their hobbies, etc. It is about understanding what motivates them as individuals and what motivates them as a team; understanding the individuals' why. And just to reiterate one more time (it is this important), when working with individuals it is not about the department; it is not about the task; it is about what is in it for each individual, and possibly what is in it for the team. If you get this right, the department and the business will flourish.

Sharing with your team

One of the easiest ways to get to know your team is by sharing part of yourself. You don't have to share personal details or your life story. Sharing part of you means keeping things appropriate. If you want to get to know your team, they will feel safe to share if you allow them to get to know you, and you sincerely want to get to know them. Remember, sharing your weaknesses as well as your strengths is a trust builder.

An interesting point about getting to know people is that not everybody is the same: one approach does not fit all. As you go through your career, you will find people behaving and responding differently to you. You may find some individuals who are very open and you get to know a lot about them; some individuals are introverts and sometimes it's like getting blood out of a stone; other individuals start off as introverts and build their confidence with you over a period of time through transactions and communication. Whoever the individuals within your team are, similar or not, you will have to adapt your communication style to meet their needs on an individual basis.

One of the best avenues that I have found for achieving this is through having regular one-to-ones with the members of my team.

One-to-ones

One-to-ones are a great way to show you are interested in individuals and for spending quality time with them. When managed well, one-to-ones will build trust, respect and loyalty from your team members. All this equates to a happy and productive workforce.

However, one of the quickest ways to lose trust and respect within your team is to arrange one-to-ones and then move them for someone or something else. Yes, there will be emergencies, and when these happen the meeting must be rescheduled, but it *must* be an emergency and not an everyday occurrence. By constantly shifting someone's one-to-one, you will give them the message that they are not important – what a great way to kill trust, respect and loyalty from them.

Another way of making a one-to-one an empty gesture is by holding the meeting and then constantly clock watching, checking your phone for emails, or simply not giving the individual the time and attention they deserve.

One-to-ones are about giving and receiving feedback. In addition to this, they are a great opportunity to reflect on what has been achieved (or not), how it's been achieved, and, of course, the all-important "What is next?" All this takes some preparation, but the meeting doesn't have to be long-winded and time-consuming. It does have to be meaningful with quality outcomes.

You will read when you get to the 'Time Management' chapter that there are some fundamental rules to managing meetings, and these must also be applied to one-to-ones. One of the key rules is never go over your time limit. If you set a one-to-one for 30 minutes, then you finish at the very latest after 30 minutes. You do not take your team member over that time, otherwise it's another indication that you don't respect them or their time.

One-to-ones are about sharing, giving and taking: perfect opportunities to build trust and respect with your team, but the trust and respect building should not be assigned only to these times. They should be an ongoing natural occurrence.

GIVING FEEDBACK

Giving positive feedback is easy and most people enjoy it, although most people do not give positive or negative feedback well. The primary objective of delivering any piece of feedback is to allow the recipient to improve on the subject discussed, whether the feedback is positive or negative.

I have witnessed over and over again managers (including very senior managers) giving feedback badly. One of the fundamental mistakes is when a manager either tells someone that they are not good at the job, or they say, "You were very good today." There's absolutely no point in this feedback. How can the recipient improve upon their role if the provider of the feedback is not specific?

Ensure that when you give feedback it *is* specific, for example: "The way you managed Mr Smith's complaint was outstanding. You were courteous and responsive and sought a solution quickly." The takeaway for the recipient is that their attitude and behaviour was positive, and they can now mirror those attributes when dealing with the next customer.

Equally when the feedback is negative: "Julie, when dealing with Mr Smith's complaint, you sounded very uninterested in his issue. You asked him to repeat his issue four times, and when he asked if you should take notes in order to remember it, you raised your voice and blamed his accent for your misunderstanding. You referred to him as Mr Jones on three occasions, made no attempt to resolve the issue whilst you had Mr Smith on the phone and did not agree a call-back time. Furthermore, you did not call Mr Smith back within the service levels that have been agreed and are part of the process."

Again, the recipient of this feedback has very specific points to take away.

Remember delete, distort and generalisation? Aim to get buy-in from the recipient and get their take on how they can improve on the incident in question.

Feedback should not be left too long before being discussed. Always remember the old adage of 'Praise in public and punish in private'. It is important that feedback is delivered within the right environment with the right audience and within a timely manner. If the incident is severe, then a one-to-one is an ideal forum to give and receive feedback.

FEEDBACK PROCESS

1. Isolate the incident that is to be discussed, including within this the behaviour and outcomes

When giving negative feedback, it is always a requirement to remove any personal emotions you may associate with the incident. Be very clear on what happened, the chain of events that led to the incident and the outcome, rather than what should have happened, or, when giving positive feedback, be clear on what went well.

2. Clarify the facts

Isolate the incident and be very clear what the facts are. There should be no assumptions made.

If you have received feedback from someone else, they must be able to back up their report. Ensure you never go into a meeting with the statement: "Someone told me, and they do not want me to say who they are." All feedback from external sources must be based on fact. Remember, everyone will delete, distort and generalise.

Always ask your team member for their take on the series of events. Where possible, tie down the facts. It will be difficult for your member of staff to separate their emotions from the incident.

3. Discuss the changes or duplication required

Working with your team member, discuss what changes must be made, or what the duplication should look like. Engage your team member.

4. Confirm the way forward

Again working with your team member, put in place a plan on how to carry forward the changes or duplication. This should be agreed by all parties involved.

Making you mark with internal promotions

A word of caution: it is often difficult to move from being a mate to a managerial role successfully, and I write this through experience. In a previous role I started as a manager of two individuals and was soon promoted to manager of 30+. Very naïvely I thought that I could make changes quickly, and some might say (I'm in complete agreement) that those changes were detrimental to team motivation.

One of the first changes I made was to formalise a lunch hour and get individuals to rota on to lunch cover. I thought that the fact I was friends with some of the 30+ individuals meant that this transition would be seamless – my, was I wrong! The idea was good, the execution was shocking, and the outcome was horrendous. I had created a situation that involved inviting other managers to support it and help with the uproar that I had caused.

Never, ever overestimate peer loyalty when it comes to management. Your mate to manager role must be carried out with understanding and empathy for the team that you are now managing, and this means almost starting from the beginning again getting to know them. Strange as this may seem, you are their manager now: there are different dynamics taking place, and a different mindset in place for you and, I suspect, for them. As well as assertively delivering processes and procedures, giving instructions, delegating, telling, etc., you must now deliver communications that your team may not like without getting caught up in the gossip and whinging.

I would highly recommend that you don't do as I did and go in with a bull-in-a-china-shop mindset. I made my mark; it was not a good one. Stop, breathe and ask yourself:

- What is my goal?

- What is the win/win (assertive)?

- How might this be received by the team?

- Do I have any wriggle room to change things?

Get your team's buy-in – selling the sizzle, not the sausage

Great managers know how to engage their team. They know how to get the best from the team, and they do this by 'selling the sizzle and not the sausage'. And by that I mean they sell the benefits of carrying out a particular task or project rather than the functionality. This is an old sales' methodology: sales people promote the benefits to the buyer not what the product does.

Let's put this into context: you want a member of your staff to take on additional work. This will increase productivity, expand your product or service offering, save you time and increase bottom-line. Everything that you have just read is the sausage.

Now to selling the sizzle. You will want to emphasise to your team member what they will get from taking on the additional work, which must be relevant to them. What will motivate them? Is it that they will learn something new? Get exposure to new systems? Will the work give them greater contact with senior management? And so forth. Find out from one-to-ones what makes the individual tick and then gain their buy-in. Remember, it is their why not yours that will get their buy-in.

The team's buy-in benefits you

By taking the time to work with your team member and find out what will motivate them to carry out a great job, you build up trust and respect on both sides, yours and theirs. When an individual is included and their opinion and ideas are sought, it allows them to grow not just in terms of their skillset, but also in confidence. As they see their opinions and ideas are being listened to (even if not necessarily used), they will want to do a better job and contribute more and more, investing effort into the outcome.

Over time they will prove that they are delivering at least what you require, and at best exceeding your expectations, and you as a manager will reap the benefits of this. If delivery is as required or, even better, at a greater quality, clients will return for more services. If clients are returning, business is increasing, therefore bottom-line is increased.

Internal clients

This is also true when you are delivering a service or product to internal clients. If you and your team are providing a constantly improving service to your internal clients, this should be making their roles easier. After all, you don't want to be giving a service or product to your clients that makes their jobs more difficult.

Individual development needs

There may be an urge for you to continue to carry out tasks and procedures that you have always carried out. This must change when you are promoted into a managerial position. It does not mean that you immediately stop carrying out your previous work; it does mean that you need to consider what you can hand over and what you retain. This is not cherry picking, choosing what you like and what you don't like; this is a logical process. Look at your responsibilities and tasks and see if there is someone better within the team to carry them out. Do not be tempted to think that there is no one who can step up and carry out the tasks and responsibilities as well as you can. After all, someone has given you an opportunity. Pay it forward.

There is an ideal opportunity within one-to-ones to discuss with individuals their development requirements and your plans to expand their roles (possibly through delegation).

This is one of those crucial points where you need some consideration and preparation prior to bringing up the subject of delegation, which will be covered in more detail in Chapter 11 – 'Delegation'.

One of the temptations within a managerial role, particularly when you are new to management, is not to commit to anything, generally through lack of confidence or preparation, which gives you the excuse not to delegate. With your staff that may manifest itself as non-commitment to their development needs. You may choose to use excuses such as: "The team does not have the skillset"; "I do not have the time to train them"; "Their standards are not as high as mine" and so forth.

The other side of the coin is that you fight for everything for everyone. Choose your battles to win the war. This demonstrates that you are taking a mature and professional stance concerning the team's wants and wishes. You need to be professional on your take on this and review what the positive outcome and impact will be for the individual and the return on investment for the business, setting expectations of what is possible and what is a no-go. It is better to set an expectation that the recipient does not want to hear than string them along and never deliver. You will gain respect for your honesty.

Setting expectations

One of my first managerial roles was as manager of one other person. I remember my behaviour hadn't progressed from mate to manager: I still behaved as if I was in a more junior role. I had the mindset of a staunch Union leader:

fight for everything and agree to everything; the Step-Up Mindset wasn't there.

If my team member asked for something, without thinking it through I would say, "Leave this with me and I will check." I believe I became a great big thorn in my manager's side. I also believe (I didn't have the conviction to ask for feedback) that I had the reputation of being a whinger: "I want, I need", etc.

Hindsight being a marvellous thing (wish I could bottle it), I realise this was part of a learning curve, and my point of learning from this was that I had to set expectations and be assertive in my delivery of those expectations. I had to have a clear understanding of what could and could not be achieved, and if it could be delivered to what level and standard (and often cost), what I wanted (my why) and what I thought would be beneficial to the department and business.

As a young manager, you may not be thinking that far ahead or considering the consequences. The TRUST template that you will visit in detail later in the book will assist you with this way of thinking.

CHAPTER REFLECTION AND ACTION – IT IS ALL ABOUT THE TEAM

When you think of a good manager, consider their interaction with their team.

You will recognise that they share good and constructive feedback. They carry this out at the appropriate times and within the appropriate environments.

Consider a situation that you would like to have given feedback on.

- What was the incident?

- What were the facts? Ignore the hearsay.

- Take out the personality and focus on the actions.

- What would you like the outcome to have been?

- How would the individual have been able to meet this outcome?

Now you have a process for giving feedback, ensure that you carry it out at appropriate times.

If you have not already done so, set up recurring one-to-ones with your team. It is the ideal opportunity to discuss feedback.

CHAPTER 8

TASK MANAGEMENT

As the service provider or product provider you will have more than just your offering to consider.

Within the arena of task lies your customers, both internal and external. After all, if you have agreed to provide someone with something, they are you customer. Yes, even you own staff become your customers if you say yes to providing them with something, and it makes sense that if you are providing a service or a task, it leads to a positive outcome. There is a need to ensure that the work carried out by yourself and your team has a positive impact on the business.

Within my coaching practice I often come across managers, including senior managers, who when challenged for a reason why they carry out a particular task, reply, "It is how it's always been done."

The phrase 'it is how it's always been done' is a bugbear of mine. I recall when working for a large investment bank, part of my role was the responsibility for collating and distributing a weekly report. This would take 4 to 5 hours of my time each week: I prepared the report on a Friday to be distributed on Monday.

In all the time I carried this out, I never received feedback or questions from any of the recipients. After some time within the role, there was an occasion when I was unable to distribute the report on two consecutive weeks, and not one person asked for it! I never spent any further time on that report, and when I left the role 18 months later I'd still had no one ask what happened to it.

For me, this was 'it's what you have always done' in play. Without giving it any thought, I had been stealing many hours of my week to deliver something that had absolutely no impact on individuals or the business.

Impact on customer

If you're in a current role, it is worth the time and effort to carry out an audit of tasks and processes to ensure that they still have a positive impact for the recipients. This may include asking the question, "Can you deliver something better?", although I would recommend not asking the individual who carries out the task. They may have an emotional tie to the task and feel that they are producing something of great quality. Equally, they may fear if the task was to be removed that potentially their job would no longer be required.

It's worth going directly to the recipient of the service or the product. This may be a long-term project, but it does not have to happen within the first week of a new role. In fact, I would recommend that you understand what your department and your team are about and build trust and respect before diving in and making unnecessary waves that will potentially demotivate the team. Remember, motivate rather than coming across with a bull-in-a-china-shop approach!

Remaining within the impact on customer thought process, one other potential benefit of carrying out the task audit exercise is that it will give you direct exposure and communication with the customers. This ideally will lead to building a strong relationship to work with your customers rather than for or even against them.

Asking your customers for their opinion and input will show them that you respect and value their opinion and input. This will lead to a level of trust. Building trust opens up a whole new avenue of possibilities and opportunities for all parties involved. When you suggest and recommend new services or products, or even an improvement on the current service or product, your customer is going to be more open to suggestions and input. Your relationship ideally will look more like a partnership than a traditional master (client) and servant (supplier) scenario.

Making mistakes

One of the great advantages of building strong relationships with your customers is that they will know what to expect from you. When those expectations are met, and ideally exceeded, you will find that they will allow for the occasional hiccup. The key to resolving mistakes which directly impact your customer is to admit openly there's been an error and either go back with a solution or work with them to resolve the issue.

I have heard from both my customers and others' customers that when mistakes are faced and resolved, it tends to build more trust and respect between them and the team involved. I also know of customers who have finished relationships with teams who've tried to hide their mistakes.

The task itself

From earlier in the chapter, you know one of the first areas you need to ensure as a manager is that your resources are being used effectively and efficiently. This can be carried out through auditing the tasks and processes and dealing directly with the customers, all with the input of your team. Remember buy-in!

Another check or audit you may wish to consider is the value of the task. I don't mean in terms of financial value, although of course this is a definite consideration; I mean you must consider the value to the customer and the use of resources to garner that value.

I shared earlier the story of the weekly report that no one put any level of importance on. I wonder what would have happened if I had taken the time to engage the recipients of the report and ask what they got from it. What would they want from the report? What would increase the value of the report for them? Would that have made a difference? I genuinely don't know as I didn't ask.

If you understand the value of the task you're delivering to your customers, you can step back and analyse what input is required. From those measurements, you can work out if your resources, e.g. your team members, time, budget, equipment, etc., are effectively being utilised. It may be that you are giving the client more than they need and can release some resources for better use. It may be that the client requires something a little different, or a lot different, in which case you can start to plan the resource requirements to deliver on this. It may be that there is no value to the customer and therefore you can take all the resources and place them somewhere else, providing a better service or product to other customers or a new product or service to your existing customer.

Setting expectations is vital and must be shared with your customers. Ignoring the outcomes of audits is not an option. Arrange meetings with your customers to discuss the suggested changes formally. During these audit meetings it is crucial to discuss all the options available. When reducing a service to your customer, ensure that you sell the sizzle. After all, would you not be very annoyed if your supplier was to reduce or stop delivering a service to you without any explanation of what is in it for you?

Exploring with your team the value of the tasks will get their buy-in (or not) for delivery. It is worth using your meetings to reset anything that you can't deliver on. There may also be an opportunity to set new expectations for the customers, but whether that is providing a lesser service or a greater service can only be defined once you've carried out some audits.

I'm sure there are many more audits that you may wish to consider for yourself.

Deadlines

It is worth considering as you go through the audits of the tasks and resources being used what deadlines can be altered or implemented.

As you audit your internal processes and tasks, you should be considering whether the process is the most efficient. Can it be amended to make it more streamlined and therefore save time? Can the process be automated? If it can be automated, it is worth investing in research and software to carry this out, which is why it is always advisable to have a good relationship with your ICT department. Remember your key and critical contacts?

Wherever possible, old and new processes should have clear deadlines, with hard outcomes and milestones set out within the process. The deadlines and milestones should always have buffer time included within them to accommodate any emergencies or unforeseen circumstances whilst still being able to deliver the service or product to deadline. Never disappoint your customer or stress out your staff with unfeasible deadlines.

A rule of thumb I have lived by for some time when setting deadlines with customers is to under-promise and over-deliver. If I believe that something will take me three days, I will say to the customer that I will get it to them at the end of day five. When I deliver at the end of day three or during day four, the customer is delighted. However, one thing you must keep in mind is not to look unprofessional by under-promising and over-delivering by a ridiculous amount. Frequently overestimating and delivering way in advance of your agreed deadline will infer that you do not know your products or services, or that you do not understand your resource pool. Neither is a professional approach or reputation builder.

Task upsell

As you work your way through the task audits, ask yourself whether there is a service or product you're providing that you can extend. Often, because of the open court 'this is how we've always done it' mindset, people do not consider the service they are providing. They assume, rightly or wrongly, that the customer must be happy with it because they've had no feedback. And that old cliché 'no news is good news' is used as a comfort blanket for managers.

Alice in Wonderland

I recently attended the Alice in Wonderland Experience at the Waterloo Vaults in London. I'd had an idea it was going to be different from any other show that I had been to, but oh wow, what an experience it was. I certainly wasn't expecting what was offered.

The whole delivery of the show was successful. Actually, it was more than successful, it was absolutely outstanding. The point that sticks in my mind was the fact that we walked from scene to scene and the transfers were interactive. There was a member of the cast with us at all times, engaging and encouraging interaction.

What did they do differently?

The Alice in Wonderland Experience could easily have created something that was satisfactorily delivered in the traditional format. However, what they created was an experience that was unlike any other within the theatre. Following a pack of cards theme, the guests were split into 4 suits – hearts, diamonds, clubs and spades. Each pack was taken off on a separate adventure, then all four packs met up at the Mad Hatter's Tea Party (nice upsell of cocktails for this).

If time had permitted, I would absolutely go back (and pay) to experience the other card suits' adventures and see how they differed from each other, how they were similar and how they added up to the whole experience.

What difference can you make to inspire your customers to enquire about your other services and offerings?

RECOGNISING VALUE ADD AND POSITIVE IMPACT

What is value add and what is positive impact?

Value add and positive impact are quite different, with one being measurable and the other not.

Positive impact cannot be measured. It is not tangible, it can only be demonstrated through behaviour. It is where you deliver a feel-good factor to your customer; it's an emotional connection and makes your customer feel great about working with you.

Value add is where you have a contract (I am referring to both a verbal and written contract) with a hard outcome delivering a product or service. When it comes to delivery, you give value add by giving the customer over and above what the contract states or you have agreed. This may be something as simple as providing an additional report or adding another part that the customer will use, but as long as the customer is getting something in addition to what was agreed, you are *adding value*.

Positive impact and value add generally go hand-in-hand. However, in my experience it is often the case that you have to highlight the value add to the customer. This is not to be carried out in an arrogant manner: you have gone the extra mile and it cost £x, so much time, so many resources, etc. Highlighting value add to your customer should not be delivered in an 'it is all about me and my team' manner as that form of delivery takes away any positive impact. In fact, it can leave the customer frustrated and annoyed that you went the extra mile without involving them and then whinged about it.

To highlight that you have given value add, you again need to sell the sizzle.

Selling the sizzle

Think through what the benefits are to the customer and not the functionality the value add gives them. You have to present this as a customer-centric offering and not as a 'how great am I?' offering. Believe me, if this is delivered correctly, your customer will know how the value add and positive impact will benefit them.

Measuring value add

Value add should have very clear measurements in terms of return on investment for you and your department.

I sometimes hear from clients, more often than not from middle level managers, that giving value add only encourages customers to want more (I would say that 80% of those saying this are talking about internal customers). This gives you an indication of these manager's attitudes towards their customers and the level of service they provide: the very best for them is to deliver their agreed goals, and I suspect more than likely they do not meet the agreed goals every time.

This is a key point that we work on throughout the coaching relationship.

Following a statement like: "Giving value add only encourages customers to want more", I work through a particular exercise with these managers. They consider what would happen if the customers were in a position to source the service they provide from elsewhere, and the bottom-line is that their department would be no longer be required.

Many years ago I worked with a company who centralised their services within the UK. ICT, HR, Finance, Marketing and other departments were run from a central location with one central budget. This didn't work for the company as a whole, and therefore the CEO entrusted the individual departments to manage their own budgets. This worked so much better for them, particularly those departments which were geographically based outside of the central location.

Then there were further complaints that the central services, specifically the ICT department, were offering a less than acceptable service. The CEO had clearly heard too many times how some central services were underperforming, and he informed all the departments that they could measure the internal services as if they were engaging with an external supplier, the premise being that if the 'customer' department could receive better services for the same cost or less, then they could use an external supplier. The CEO also informed ICT of this new change to process and procedure with the very clear message: improve your service or the service will be eradicated.

Nine months after the initial change to process and challenge to the ICT team, 40% of the overall ICT budget spend was being channelled externally. The impact on the internal department: no improvement to the service, even though they were now servicing a smaller customer base.

Eighteen months after the initial change to the process and challenge to ICT, there was no internal ICT department. The service was being outsourced for a smaller budget and greater level of satisfaction. Some employees were TUPEd over; the ICT manager was managed out of the role.

There are many ways of measuring value add, remembering value add is tangible:

- customer feedback;

- customer complaints;

- increased sales (including internal);

- introduction of new and improved services;

- increased charges with no loss to customer base.

CHAPTER REFLECTION AND ACTION – TASK MANAGEMENT

Managing a department is like managing your own business: you need to ensure it has energy and momentum. If you were to step back and take a helicopter view of your department and services, what would the answer be to the following questions?

- How valuable are the services supplied to your clients?

- What questions would you need to ask to find out what the customers believe?

- What would you change to create a positive impact for your customers?

- What would value add look like to your top three customers?

- Where is the chink (the bottleneck, the weakest link, etc.) in production?

- Where can your offering and service be streamlined?

- What can be automated?

- If you were to increase your charges for your product, what changes would you make to your offering?

- What one change would have the biggest impact on delivering a great service?

CHAPTER 9

SKILLSET – THIRD COMPONENT TO THE STEP-UP MINDSET

Having a greater understanding of the importance of positive attitude and action based behaviour will increase your chances of success, but attitude and behaviour alone will not mean success. In order to take success further, you need to be good at what you do. Delivering the great will require more than 'wanting to do it' or 'having a go at it'. What will increase your chances of success is a rounding of a great attitude and behaviour with the skillset to carry out the task and a knowledge of how to carry it out correctly.

If you have a job specification for an existing role, it will give you an idea of the skills that have been required in your role in the past as well as what someone believes are needed to grow the role further. Unless you're in a repetitive or highly processed role, your job will holistically grow as time goes on, and your skillsets will progress with those changes. If your skillset does not change, you will be left behind in the job market.

Along with your knowledge of what is required to carry out your job successfully, I would put the three top skillsets as: communication, self-management and team management (to include productivity and team morale).

This is the time to be very honest with yourself and reflect on what skillset is required and where your skillset currently is. Where possible, seek feedback from others who know the role, asking what skills are important for the success of the role. This will be an indicator of which of your existing skills you should improve and enhance, or even what new skills you need. Ideally by this time, if you are currently in the new role, you will have an understanding of it and be able to prioritise which of the skills you need for the greatest immediate impact.

If you are looking to progress into a managerial role, look at job specifications on job websites and review what is being asked for.

Many of the skills required, e.g. technical, finance, ICT, marketing, etc., are blended with the soft skills: communication, assertiveness, time management, team building, and tools and methodologies to assist you in your day-to-day running of the department, the tasks and yourself. Remember: self, task and team.

The following chapters will give you an insight into some of the skills that you will require in your management role. This will give you a greater foundation to build upon as you progress through your career. In addition to this, you will find descriptions, information, processes, tools and methodologies that will help you become a better manager.

The first of these is:

COMMUNICATION

Empires have been built or razed to the ground because of good or bad communication.

When was the last time you were upset or annoyed at work? What would have made it right? Would it have been someone being more explicit with their instructions? Would it have been if you had been more explicit with your instruction?

Communication is vital to your success as a manager or someone who is working towards a management role.

In fact, great communication is vital for all parts of life, regardless of role.

You will, in your life as a manager, be required to 'clean up' team problems both internally and externally. Being a great communicator will take you 75% of the way there. The other 25% is a mix of understanding and delivery.

COMMUNICATION STYLES

Just like the earlier management styles, your communication should be flexible. It is important to have the know-how to recognise which style best suits the situation and the audience. Looking on the Internet, you will find many communication styles, but in this book you are going to review and reflect on four very different but simple styles that will deliver effective outcomes. There is no one better style or right style. The right style is the one that suits the situation.

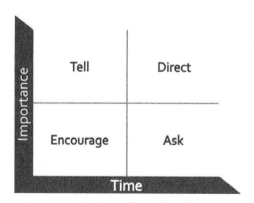

Let's look at the following four styles:

Tell – no time, high importance

This is based on the task management style and suits the delivery of legislation and process installations. Where there is a direct instruction to be delivered, this is what is required of you and how you are going to achieve it.

This style requires assertive delivery with no or minimal room for negotiation. It is a 'do as I say' approach, without the bully tactics or aggressive delivery.

Direct – more time, high importance

This style is used when there is a high level of importance assigned to the task, but there is time for the manager to work closely with the team to coach and direct with a clear and hard outcome. The outcome is often non-negotiable and generally has high impact on external influences, e.g. clients, other teams, auditors, etc., usually with a long lead time for delivery.

This style requires clear direction and outcomes with the opportunity for the recipients to work on possible alternatives on how to meet these.

Ask – more time, less importance

This is a great opportunity to allow others to develop new skillsets and ideally increase motivation (attitude) and outcomes (behaviour). It is generally considered safe for the assigned individual(s) to work autonomously to enable them or the team to respond back with solutions and outcomes, often with little input from the manager. The manager may use this as a development opportunity to assist the individual(s) whilst not owning the learnings or outcomes.

Encourage – less time, less importance

This is a great opportunity for a manager to develop an individual's (and their own) attitude and behaviour towards deadlines. Where there is a task to carry out and little risk with regards to the outcome or the possibility of late delivery, this allows the individual to hone their time management skills.

Getting to grips with these four simple styles will give you a clear approach to getting the best out of your team.

BEHAVIOURAL TYPES

There are three behavioural types: submissive, assertive and aggressive. Delivery of these and the management styles will be crucial to success.

For this part, you will consider the pros and cons to each style and think about when and where they may be used.

Assertive style

A great rule of thumb (and rules are written to be broken) is that you always aim to work within the assertive mode. This mode has a primary objective of win/win: you get what you want, and the other party gets what they want.

This often involves give and take and striking a balance when dealing with others. Assertive is a great position to start most (if not all) communications. Your delivery will be confident with an even tone and pitch, assured and relaxed body language and use of the words 'we', 'us', etc.: an attitude of dual wins.

There will be times when you will be assertive without a possible win for the other parties: introducing legislation, Health and Safety, and important tasks with no time. The delivery remains the same, and of course you explain the reasons behind the lack of movement on your part.

Submissive style

There is a time and place to use this style, often when you have no strong feeling either way for the outcome and therefore your input is minimal. This style of behaviour can be categorised as lose/lose, which is difficult for the other party when they see you as fundamental to the success. They may also have a lot riding on the success of the outcome.

Your delivery may be seen as nervous: quiet and low tone and pitch, hunched shoulders, head down and little to no eye contact, use of the words 'OK', 'sorry', etc. Your attitude says, "A lose for me as I will do whatever you want, and lose for you as you will get nothing more than asked for, if that".

Be careful with this style. Used too often and you may be regarded as a walkover; easy; a doormat; someone who cannot think or hold their own corner.

Aggressive style

There is never a place for this style.

This is when you want what you want without any consideration for others. In fact, you may even take some pleasure in tightening the thumb screws even when you have received what you wanted.

Your delivery will be harsh: loud and angry tone and pitch, large and stiff body language, use of the words 'you', 'I want', etc. Your attitude says, "A win for me and lose for you".

Using this style will not endear you to others: you will be considered a bully.

Remember the good, bad and ugly story? Which of these styles would motivate you? Which of these styles would you want your manager to demonstrate?

Have something worthwhile to be heard

Now you know which management and communication style is required for different situations and scenarios, you have a positive attitude and are demonstrating assertive behaviour. Have something worthwhile to say.

To communicate, you need to be heard. Before you're heard, you need to know what you are saying is worthwhile for the other party to hear. Whatever and however you communicate, the success of the message will heavily rely on who is receiving it *and* what they want to take away from it.

COMMUNICATING WITH WHOM?

Team

Who is your team made up of? Not names, think roles. What is important to the team? What is the team interested in? What will support them in their individual and team successes?

What your team needs to hear is what is happening at a company level (big picture), how this impacts them, their why, what and when. Knowing the big picture and how as a team they are expected to support this, understanding what part they play and buying into their contribution, should bring the team together, but this will only be true if the message is delivered and received correctly. Once all is said and done, the team requires praise for a great job and constructive feedback for underperformance and non-delivery.

Where changes are being considered or executed within the company and the team, the communication should be carried out face to face and delivered assertively.

Individuals

What is each individual's area of expertise and interest? If you are talking directly with someone from Finance, you can bet a key concern of theirs will be money related. If talking to Human Resources, you can bet a key concern of theirs will be employee related, and so forth. That is not to say that someone from Finance is not interested in other areas, or HR is only interested in people-specific communication. As you will know, most, if not all people need to have a knowledge or keen interest in areas of the business other than their own immediate role.

Stopping to think about your team as individuals and what is of interest to them is a key point in being a great communicator. Equally, knowing why each team member is working within your team is essential to the team's (and your) success. If you understand your team's personal motives for working, you will ideally support them with this, and in turn you will have a happier and more motivated workforce. As always, the interest in them must be genuine and authentic. Extracting information must be carried out through asking, sharing and acknowledging your team and the individuals within the team. One-to-ones are the ideal environment for this.

What is worthwhile for the individuals in your team to listen to and act upon? What is it you want to tell them? What should they hear? What do they want to hear? As a manager, you will need to remind individuals of the goals and results and the part they played within these. Your team members must receive recognition for good work and feedback on what needs to be changed. They too must know whom their critical relationships are with, and the best way for them to discover this is to allow them to find out for themselves.

Individuals like, need and positively respond to the big picture sharing. How do they fit into the team? What is their contribution and how does this work for the company strategy? This must include the uncomfortable: knowing the truth is better than guessing the gossip. Being honest even when the communication is uncomfortable to deliver and hear will build trust and respect.

Peers

Is your objective to be a better performing manager with a better performing team? If yes, it is important to know who your peers on the other teams are and build sustainable relationships with them. Who are your key contacts and who are your critical contacts? You will know from an earlier chapter that critical contacts are those who depend on you for their role to be completed well and those whom you rely on to ensure that you get your job completed. Key contacts are those who will smooth the way to carrying out your service with little or no interruption.

Your peers who have a connection with your offering and your team are the ones who must be best informed about all the things that will lead to success for you, the business, the team and, of course, themselves. Both key and critical relationships should be kept abreast of what is happening, what has happened and any future plans.

Manager

Reflect on your manager. What is their preferred and most prominent management style? Which communication style do they most readily choose? What interests them?

If they are a task manager then their interest will primarily be on task progress; if a people manager then their interest will be in people. How do they manage you? Are they detailed or high level with their communication? Do they micro-manage you or are they hands off? Are they somewhere in between? Knowing the answers to these questions will give you a greater understanding of them and how best to approach them. Whilst being authentic, consider how to respond to them (just them) by mirroring the style that they are demonstrating.

Always remember, individuals will demonstrate attitude and behaviour based on the current situation. As situations change, so will their behaviour. Therefore, it is crucial that you do not label someone and only communicate in one style with them. It will be a wasted engagement opportunity and you will not meet your objective. Be flexible, work towards recognising the different styles and responding accordingly.

Managing your manager

Your manager will benefit from you managing your engagements with them. This is not a deceitful strategy; this is a thought-through process that is delivered assertively with a win/win objective.

In preparation for engagements with your manager, always look to pre-empt their questions and provide the information before the questions are asked. Part of this will come from experience of working with your manager, part of this will be in your preparation. Managers want and need to know what is happening. They need to be aware of something they may be asked about, or if something has gone wrong, they need to know the bad news as well.

You should absolutely give time to consider managing your manager. Share with your manager your progress to date and future tasks alongside the deadlines. Let them see you are managing your own workload and take away the need for them to spoon-feed you. You may meet the micromanager who will do this regardless, but the benefit of being knowledgeable about what is happening and has happened will be that you'll be able to set expectations. In addition to this, being proactive will give you practice for your next role or manager.

Customers

Considering your communication with your customers is a similar process to considering your engagement with your manager. There is a need to manage their expectations, inform them of past achievements and future plans, but the content will be different.

With your customers, you will inform them of past actions that impact them (not your department or individuals) and future plans that involve them. There is also a requirement to ensure you choose the best way to communicate with customers. How do they communicate with you? What communication style do they most readily choose? What interests them? Do they like guidance? Do they like to hear the latest on the industry changes and progress?

Find this out through authentic networking.

EFFECTIVE FORMS OF COMMUNICATION

In an ideal world, we would always communicate face to face. The real world dictates that this is not always convenient due to time and distance. With the technology options we have on offer, there are now many forms of communication, each of them having their own advantages and disadvantages. It is important to choose the right form of communication, taking into account time, distance, importance and objective.

Emails

Emails have become such an important part of everyday communication, we tend to use them as naturally as we would speak to someone. What is not often taken into account when using this medium is the simple and yet extremely important fact that emails do not transmit intended body language, tone and pitch. The words that you use within your emails do not express the emotion you assign to the words, and what often happens is the receiver of the email assigns their own current emotion at the time of reading. This can result in a disconnect between the intended message and the message being read, sometimes with the message being received in a far more negative way than you intended. You will rarely hear of anyone complaining about a positive misinterpretation of an email. With this in mind, ensure that all your emails deliver the message in the tone you were looking to communicate.

Emails should not be used to replace face to face meetings or telephone conversations. Have you ever heard anyone saying, "His management style is outstanding – his emails are inspiring, they so get everything done"? I wouldn't have thought so. Emails should not be used as a way of passing over your responsibilities either.

I have worked in many companies where there is a blame culture, with managers and staff feeling they have to cover themselves all the time. In these instances, this is generally camouflaged by saying, "I'll put it in an email" which can translate to, "I sent an email, my job was done. This is your fault". Come on, people, stop the blame culture and use emails as a form of communication and not an arse-covering tool.

Holding emails

One of the most frustrating points of working with emails is sending out a message which requires a response, receiving no response and not knowing if it has even been viewed. You can put on a delivery notification, but personally I find them incredibly rude and frustrating, and many others I have spoken to with regards to them also find them rude. Someone opening an email does not mean it has been read. There needs to be a follow-up to emails you receive that require a response or action from you.

Often it is not rudeness that is the problem when we do not respond to emails, it is time management or self-management. An easy work around this is to send a 'holding email': not an auto response, but a personal message that thanks the sender for the email, acknowledges receipt and gives a timescale expected for response. Ensuring that you respond within the timescale given really drives home a message of responsiveness and trustworthiness – you will recall these as two of the attributes associated with being a great manager. You need to be seen as 'on the ball', the real world dictates that we give an instant response, but it is not always possible to meet this. Holding emails confirms to the sender that their message has been received and acknowledged.

Face to face

This is the easiest, clearest and cleanest of the mediums to get your message across to the receiver. They are then able to match what you are saying to your body language, tone and pitch to make a subconscious decision as to whether they believe the message.

As you will recall, the message you are sending will be distorted, deleted and generalised by the receiver. In a face to face communication, it is easier to find out through asking questions the receiver's take on your message, although asking "Do you understand?" or "Have you got that?" should not give you reassurance they really have understood. The answer will only confirm they have understood what their interpretation of the message is – deleted, distorted and generalised.

Telephone

The receiver of your communication will put more emphasis on the tone and pitch of your voice as they will not be able to read your body language. However, digesting the information will be the same as face to face: the receiver will distort, delete and generalise. When you are communicating by phone, you have the benefit of asking questions for clarification, which is a more fluid communication than email. The telephone should be used when face to face is not possible.

Acknowledge your internal conversations

It is important to recognise that in order to be a great communicator with others, you need to be communicating well with yourself, and this includes using positive language even when things are not going your way.

Self-communication is another key component of success. Being able to talk to yourself using positive language that motivates you is a must. The negative way we often talk to ourselves and the things we say we would not even say to someone we didn't like, and all this negative internal talk can lead to physical manifestations and play a large part in how we respond to others.

Can you recall a time when talking to someone that you knew instinctively things were not right with them? What was it about them that let you know how they were feeling before you asked any questions? Body language, tone, pitch and the language that the individual was using would have played a great part in your coming to that conclusion.

When talking with someone, you ask, "How are you?" and their response is, "Not too bad". How does it make you feel? I would have thought if you were to spend too much time with them they would kill your positive energy. Negative people are mood hoovers. It is so much easier to suck light-hearted, positive energy out of a room of people than it is to suck heavy, negative energy. Ensure as a manager that you consider the language that motives you and in turn motivates your team.

The 'not too bad' manager

Can you imagine how demotivating it is when a staff member asks their manager, "How are you?" and the response is, "Not too bad"? How do you think the team member may respond to the "Not too bad"?

There is a very good chance that they will respond negatively and feel in themselves that they may be not too bad too, and so now you have the manager feeling not too bad and you have a team member feeling not too bad. How long before this not too bad feeling impacts the rest of the team? All of a sudden you have a whole team feeling not too bad, and the output becomes not too bad.

Not too bad, as you know, really means: "I'm not feeling too good about things, but I am trying to put on a brave face. However, I want to mope around and be negative." The outcome is an unmotivated and under-performing team. The 'not too bad' will suck all the energy out of them.

What does positive language sound like? Positive language is recognising that things are not always going to go according to plan, you're not always going to feel 100% happy and healthy, sometimes you may need to accept that things are not going to go your way, goalposts will move and you need to move with them. Positive language is taking all of the above, and other situations which are not perfect, acknowledging that things are not right, learning from them and turning them into positives. Then you can start or continue to be better managers using language that motivates and creates positive energy to drive you forward.

INFLUENCING OTHERS

What you can control and what you can influence are two sides of the same coin. Can you control others' behaviour? No. Can you control what is happening outside of your department? No. Outside of your team? No. Can you control the goalposts being moved by your clients? No. Can you control your team? No. What you can do is have some level of influence over how things happen and how things are perceived, and this is where a great manager will come into their own.

You may take from the above paragraph that you have very little control over many things, and that's true. One positive thought to keep in mind is that you do have control over yourself, and self-management will take you 60 to 70% of the way to managing your team, your tasks and your clients, not forgetting company objectives and your brand and reputation.

Believing in the message that you want to influence the other party with is crucial. And, of course, influencing others is down to great communication. What is the recipient's preferred style and how will you respond to that?

SELF-MANAGEMENT

In order to manage your team, your objectives, your tasks, the team's tasks, your manager, department objectives and more, including deadlines, your peers, and your clients, you must be confident in self-management.

The key areas in self-management:

- your attitude and motivation;

- your communication delivery and engagement;

- your behaviours and outcomes;

- your time management.

We will look at self-management more in Chapter 11.

YOUR ATTITUDE AND MOTIVATION

Whilst your attitude alone will not determine success, it plays a large part in the success process. In earlier chapters you will have read of the importance of attitude, and how it is vital to have the right attitude for the right outcomes. Influencing your own attitude will result in changing your behaviours, and in return impact on outcomes.

Your attitude also plays a large part in your perceived reputation and brand.

I recall once working with two senior managers. One was the Head of Services and the other was his manager, the Director of Services. The Head of Services was a dour, gloomy and solemn person. He rarely smiled and he made communication difficult. On the few occasions that I dealt directly with him, I would leave the meeting feeling drained, depressed and exhausted.

One day, whilst having a conversation with his manager, the Director of Services, I recall that I requested some information that would involve the Director of Services having to talk with the Head of Services.

The Director of Services responded, "I don't have the energy, the want, or the will to discuss this at the moment with him. I need to do it at a later date when I'm ready to do battle."

I remember in my naivety asking, "If he is such hard work, how did he get to be Head of Services?"

The response was, "I ask the same question every time I deal with him. His promotion was before I arrived, and I very much doubt he will be here when I leave."

The Head of Services had a small team, and each and every one of them projected the same attributes as their manager: dour, gloomy, resistant. They were all shockingly bad at communication, and not one of them was particularly pleasant to work with.

What did this attitude say about both the Head of Services and the Director of Services? Their teams? How did this feed into their brand and the reputation of the individuals and their teams?

The Head of Services as well as the Director of Services and his department were made redundant within 12 months.

Had the Director had the time, energy and confidence to coach and manage the Head of Services and the impact his behaviour and attitude were having on those around him, I believe he could have saved the department. If only he had aligned his attitude to the problem in hand, to the role. However, by ignoring the situation he caused a change effect that meant he was seen as a poor manager, and so the whole team had to go as they were a hindrance to company performance.

CHAPTER REFLECTION AND ACTION – COMMUNICATION

- What is your natural management style – tell, direct, ask or encourage?

- Think of everyday situations within the workplace. Which style would suit each one best?

- What is your natural behaviour style – assertive, submissive or aggressive?

- Thinking of your critical and key relationships, what can you change to offer a structured win/win offering?

- What are you regularly communicating to your:

    o   team?

    o   peers?

    o   manager?

    o   clients?

- Is it appropriate?

- Is it too much/too little?

- How often are you giving quality time to your team in one-to-ones?

- What can you do to make this a more productive meeting?

Challenge – reduce sending emails by 20% over the coming month.

CHAPTER 10

GOAL SETTING

KNOW YOUR GOAL

As a manager of an IT department, I on several occasions (and please note, one occasion would have been too many) interviewed people who didn't know what role they were being interviewed for. These interviewees had turned up as a result of an employment agency getting in touch with them and suggesting they go for the job, with neither the agency nor the individual caring enough to ensure that they were a good match for the role. Both the agency and the individuals were taking a 'spray and pray' approach: go to enough interviews and pray someone will take them on. I didn't.

This not only reflected badly on the agency (I stopped using this agency with immediate effect), it was also detrimental to the individuals' reputations. This is not going to happen to you.

Think: are you taking the 'spray and pray' approach to your future?

Why and where

I have spoken with many coaching clients who know they have to be somewhere else, they're just not sure where and how. How motivating is it when you know you should be doing something different but do not know what or how?

I have had team members working on individual projects and goals with no idea of why or how this fitted into the bigger picture.

Time to stop

If you continue to do what you have always done, you will continue to get the results you have always had.

Now is the time to stop and breathe, and then start delivering with a Step-Up Mindset.

Time to start

Now is the time to take action. Let's get in the correct frame of mind – change attitudes, demonstrate with action, influence behaviour and deliver each and every time. Impact outcomes.

Be in the know

A lot of people, and believe me by lots I mean more than those I have met, and I have in the past been included in this statement, often start on their career journey with a vague (or no) idea of where they were going. Many will have attended university and will now be working in a role that has no correlation with their qualifications. Those who have not attended university will have started out in a role that was available rather than with a conscious career move. Individuals will wait for opportunities to present themselves before taking the plunge, or worse not recognise the opportunities and be stuck in a role that neither inspires them nor meets their needs. This is particularly true when you see the world through your 'deprived and unlucky me' glasses.

Can you recall a time when you were so unhappy with a situation that for a long time all you were able to see was that it was what you did not want? How devastating did it feel? The unhappiness, the despair, the frustration. How did this feeling impact the other areas of your life? It permeates more than just work.

Maybe you are in this place now. Are you looking for direction? Are you looking for promotion? Are you feeling out of your depth? Not knowing where to turn for the next step?

Stop and breathe.

Before you begin with the how and what, you need to know two things: the *where* and the *why.* Knowing your where and your why, you can ensure that they are congruent and in sync. Have you ever got out a map and decided your route without knowing where you wanted to be? Have you ever started a task without knowing how it would look when it was finished? Forgotten why you're doing something? Check in regularly to ensure that your where and why are still relevant and the motivators they are today.

OUTCOMES

You must be very clear of your destination and know when you have reached it. To ensure the motivation is there to work towards this goal, a very clear understanding of why is also important. That is not to say once you reach your final destination you have to stop working with that goal, nor am I saying that once you know your goal you stick with it without any thought to changing circumstances and wants as the unknown unfolds. No, what I am saying is you need to know the direction to work in, and if there are any road blocks or diversions you can re-plan, knowing again the direction you need to be facing. Or alternatively, if that destination no longer suits your goals, you know what not to be doing.

You need to TRUST that you are on the right track.

TRUSTed OUTCOMES

"Don't work harder, work smarter" is how the saying goes. One of the better clichés...

The problem with this is that a lot of managers don't know how to 'work smarter'. And, when you talk about being smart to managers, they often think SMART goals: Specific, Measureable, Achievable, Relevant and Time-bound.

Managers feel if they work with SMART objectives it will give them the edge, but if you were to challenge this you would find out that in fact it does not. For managers to 'work smarter', there is a real need to trust that the work is being carried out efficiently and effectively; that there is a framework in place, not necessarily an elaborate project map (although on some occasions, that would be ideal), but a thought-through transition plan of what is required (the goal) and what you are to deliver on (positive and tangible outcomes).

Ladies and gentleman, let me introduce you to a new goal setting methodology: TRUST.

TRUST

Imagine having the confidence to TRUST that your time and energy are being focused in the right direction, or if incorrectly, you have the ability to steer to another path. TRUST gives you the framework to carry this out.

TRUST is an acronym for:

Treasure

Resources

Understanding

Steps

Time-bound.

Why TRUST? TRUST does as it says. Following the steps (not necessarily in order) will give you the confidence to TRUST you have covered all the points needed and know you have clarity on your goals and outcomes.

T – Treasure

What is your treasure? What is your goal? What are you looking to achieve?

Your treasure must be something worth working towards. Something that *you* want to reach for. A goal that excites you and even scares you. Your treasure must also include the benefits of the goal: your why.

R – Resources

You know your treasure, now look at the resources required to meet the goal. It may be worth at this stage moving to 'T – Time-bound'. This will give you an idea of time constraints and therefore give you a better idea of resources.

However, for this exercise you will continue with R – Resources. In an ideal world, what resources would you require? In the real world, what do you have? How would you look to bridge the gap between the ideal and real world?

U – United/Understood

With any goals, when you set them it is imperative to word them clearly, followed up by a clear idea of resources required, deadlines and timelines for activities, milestones and the steps required to accomplish these.

The difference is the U in TRUST. The autonomous template is focusing your *understanding* on how the outcome will impact you. This assumes you have the authority to carry out the plan with no external support or buy-in required. The *united* template focuses on the need to ensure you and the other parties understand the big picture and all are united in the buy-in to the success.

U – is the part that binds TRUST together. This is the part that you sit back and reflect upon to ensure that you understand the goal, the various parts, the value you are bringing and the tangible outcomes - including how the goal fits into any larger projects or goals, the impact this has on you and that all parties (if there are any others) understand, agree and are united in the success of the goal.

This is particularly true when other people are required to assist and support the success of your goal. Ensuring that you have their buy-in and, more importantly where appropriate, their manager's authorisation to use the resource(s) is vital to the success.

S – Steps

You know your treasure, you know your deadline and you know your why (the benefits to you that you consider at the treasure stage). Now is the time to consider how you are going to collect your treasure.

The biggest mistake that people often make with goals is to make them so large that they freeze or fly from them. Large goals are great, if you know how and what you need to do and when you need to do it in order to achieve your goal. This is where steps come in.

Imagine for a moment that you are going to run a marathon. You would ideally break down the 26 miles and 385 yards into more manageable steps. With any goal that feels or simply is overwhelming, there is a need to make it more manageable. Assign a step-by-step approach using milestones and target dates.

T – Time-bound

Steps and time-bound go hand in hand. As you break down the steps, add a target date for completion.

You may find it easier to start at the end and work back. You know your treasure, so what is the hard deadline for delivery on this? That is your final step. What do you need to achieve prior to this? And so forth.

Remember the Law of Balance.

Delivery – under-promise and over-deliver

One area of this to consider is how you manage your time. What can you say yes or no to?

You read earlier about being assertive. This includes saying no, and where applicable offering a solution. One way of thinking about this is to have clear control of your calendar and ensure that you understand your workload, which means that when you say yes or no to a request, you are comfortable with that response.

Many new managers want to make a good impression, and as a result often take on more than they can handle. This leads to problems: either they are unable to deliver or are working all the hours possible to deliver on their promises. Or they may underestimate the time taken to complete a request and therefore miss deadlines. There is a danger that they will damage their relationship with the recipient and their own reputation, and get stressed whilst this is happening.

One method that works is to under-promise and over-deliver, which means that if you believe your request will be completed in five days, you may wish to add an additional day as a buffer. If you complete the job early then you deliver early and your customer is delighted; if not you have the additional day to complete the role without disappointing anyone.

CHAPTER REFLECTION AND ACTION – GOAL SETTING

If you know where you are going, you will know when you arrive. If you have only a vague idea of what you are working towards, your success will be fleeting. Know where you are going, and what your aim is to get there.

- Make TRUST goal setting a habit.

- Print out several copies of each TRUST sheet – united and autonomous.

- Choose your top three goals.

- Complete a form for each goal.

- Have a clearly and positively written treasure (goal).

- Have a clear understanding of your available resources.

- Ensure you understand the Law of Balance with TRUST and you have buy-in from all parties involved and have a united attitude and approach.

- Have a clear breakdown of the steps and milestones, and write these down.

- Each step and milestone must be allocated a completion time. Ensure they are all time-bound.

- Finally, take action knowing you can place TRUST in your goals.

CHAPTER 11

TIME MANAGEMENT

Time management is an excuse for not completing jobs on time, or not completing them to the required standard of excellence. It is the excuse for an unbalanced work-life ratio, or not managing a team. Time management as a phrase should be deleted from your vocabulary; it is, after all, self-management!

I am going to let you in on a secret. Are you ready for it? Be seated. This secret could fundamentally change how you think about using the time management excuse going forward.

You have exactly the same amount of hours, minutes and seconds in the day as everyone else.

It does not matter who you are, where you are, what you believe, what you think, you still have the same amount of days in a week, hours in a day, minutes in a hour and seconds in a minute as everyone else. There you go, the secret is out there.

As this is the case, how is it that some people manage their days, hours, minutes and seconds better than others?

Strengths and weaknesses

If you find something that you are good at, you will tend to enjoy carrying the task out; and as you carry it out, you will become even better at it. When you do not know something or do not enjoy carrying out a task, there can be a tendency to find other tasks (that you do enjoy) to carry out instead.

It is as important to acknowledge your strengths as your weaknesses.

Where does your strength lie? What do you enjoy doing? Are you someone who enjoys being hands-on, being practical? Do you prefer to supervise others in the doing? Do you enjoy being part of the team, or standing on the periphery and watching the team? Does your energy flow better when you are working strategically, thinking through ideas, plans, tasks? Or does it flow when you are delivering on them? What is your motivation?

In understanding your strengths, you will apply motivation and inspiration to attitude and behaviour that requires improvement. Shift your mindset to one that is ready to carry out the necessary and not just focus on the easy and enjoyable. Weaknesses should never be seen as negatives. As a manager, you must ensure that when you are talking with your team, your manager, your peers, you portray weaknesses as positives. These are areas that you work with the individuals to improve upon and expand, therefore allowing the individual (whether that be yourself or others) the opportunity to explore and grow. In return, it increases motivation, changes attitudes, influences behaviour, impacts outcomes and increases performance and productivity.

As a manager, it is important to understand not only what you believe are your areas for improvement, but also what your manager, your team, and potentially your peers and clients believe they are. Once you have this level of understanding of yourself, you can then start to analyse the behaviours that will have the greatest impact on not just your performance (although this is very important), but also your own personal confidence and pleasure.

It's simple to enjoy your role. In fact, I would be as brazen as to say it is important to love your role. I am often concerned when coachees talk about the Sunday night and Monday morning negative feelings they experience when thinking about work. When you are not doing something right or not being perceived as doing something right, that's often when you least enjoy your job. If you recognise your weaknesses and your strengths and balance these, you have gone a very long way towards enjoying work and life in general.

The more you enjoy your role, the more it grows your confidence. You relax into the role and feel more in control; you manage your time better; you may even start spending longer at work – that is, of course, until you receive a gentle (or not so gentle) prod from someone reminding you that you have a life outside of work. You are achieving more and feeling great.

Work-life balance? Get real...

You will have met individuals who work late into the evening and all weekend and then complain, "I haven't seen the children, partner, friends, family, etc." Some feel they have to work late: the company culture dictates it, promotion depends on it, income depends on it, and so forth. This is true of males and females, with or without children.

Let's be honest about the whole work-life balance concept. It is great in theory, but for most it is just that – a theory or concept and not real life.

You as a young manager have to consider what work-life balance means to you. For most, this is where you go to work for an acceptable number of hours and balance this out with your life wants: friends, family, community, hobbies, etc. For some, it is work as hard and as long as you can now, and reap the benefits of this by being more financially secure when you are older.

Culture

There are companies out there with a culture of staff starting early and staying late. Staff are expected to be there when the managers are there, or even when the managers are not. What is being proven by this culture? Is it an ego trip? Is it identity by busyness? Is it short-sighted individuals within the company laying down the law? Is there a real need within the business to have this level of attendance? Could it be that the workloads do actually require the additional effort? Should the company be considering employing additional resources? What do long days mean to performance? And more importantly, what is the sacrifice and outcome for the individuals?

This culture is being driven down by management. It is important to realise when you and/or your team members are constantly staying late at work. Is it due to heavy workloads or is there a skillset deficiency?

Realistic

Being realistic is the first task when considering work-life balance. What does it mean to you? You are responsible for your work-life balance, so do not give that responsibility to others.

Being realistic involves understanding what, if anything, you are prepared to sacrifice – remember the Law of Balance. There is a general hope that the end results will more than justify the sacrifice. The higher you climb the career ladder, the more is expected of you, and this usually translates into additional hours on the job. What will you sacrifice to accommodate this?

If you choose a job that allows you to start late and finish early, be realistic: the pay is probably not going to be that great. What are you prepared to sacrifice? What is that sacrifice worth? If you are chasing the big bucks, something has to give.

In a world where we are bombarded with economic upturns/downturns, cost of living rising, quality of life costing more, people may feel that they must invest more time in their roles. They need to be seen to be working harder and putting in the longer hours; they want to be needed, a great worker, indispensable.

If you can't carry out your role within your contractual hours as the work is so much and so important, then does it not make sense that making you redundant would be detrimental to the business? This is not realistic. Learning on the job and increasing your skillset is the way forward, not just for you, but for your team.

A senior director recently remarked in a coaching session, "If my staff are not carrying out their work in their given hours then I would query their capabilities. If they are staying late, I want something in addition to their expected output. Give me the extra, and I would reward that performance and productivity."

Work-life balance is about addressing what is important to you and how you best achieve this. It is managing your time better.

Importance and commitment

What is important for you? What will you commit to giving up? Is it worth it?

There is generally something that has to be given up when you bring something else on board. Work-life balance is about understanding and making the commitment to this. Looking for more down-time normally results in less money. Looking for more money normally results in more time in the office. Looking to start a new career requires more time in developing yourself, and less time for other areas of your life. Setting up a company – wow, that is a commitment and a real sacrifice (from experience), although the rewards can be fantastic.

There is give and take, and you need to know what yours is. Commit to your important outcomes and work towards them, but be realistic when thinking work-life balance.

Work-life balance is not an unreachable nirvana. It is about real effort on your part to understand what your nirvana looks like, and understanding and managing when things get in the way: the emergency at work that calls for immediate attention as you close down your laptop; the early morning meeting being rearranged to work around childcare. You have to be flexible for it to work for all parties, not just you or the company.

One of the greatest forces working against you is time, or more importantly, your self-management and how realistic you are with fitting everything into your day. There is the same amount of time for everyone; it's just a matter of being focused.

Stop thinking of the ideal world; start working towards your real world. Part of that is giving serious thought to your work-life balance, and remembering taking something on does mean that you give something up. It is what you choose to give up that is the tough part.

Stop thinking of the prescriptive ideal world; start working towards your own. Manage your time and your team's time better.

PROCRASTINATION – ENERGY AND CONFIDENCE THIEF

Procrastination is the slackers' playground.

Procrastination comes in many forms. The eternal thinker who never delivers to the "It's a work in progress", to the "I don't have time to do what I am doing, let alone take on new things", to the "I know I am procrastinating and doing nothing about changing it", to my old favourite "Of course I will do that" and then radio silence and hiding. Out of sight, out of mind. Score to procrastination!

Procrastination is like an illness, eating away at your energy bit by bit whilst starting to gnaw at your confidence. It gives you the time to think of the many reasons why you should not be dealing with something, or why you are unable to deal with it. Procrastination gives you barriers and justifications not to start a task, and it also gives you a bad reputation. Still, you can work at your reputation another time, right? After all, you control your reputation, and therefore you can switch on and off what people think of you.

The correct answer to the above question is no!

Procrastination can lead to individuals being prone to illness. They start to consider everything that is wrong with their job and stress that others are seeing their faults. Truth be told, after a short while those around them *will* recognise the sheer act of their procrastinating, and their demeanour and physiology. This obviously feeds into their enjoyment, or rather lack of enjoyment within their role.

When this happens, negativity takes control. Their mindset shifts from the Step-Up Mindset to whinging, "Bad things always happen to me".

The whinger mindset

The whinger's mindset will generally prove the whinger right. With the 'bad things always happen to me' mindset, they will see only the bad in every situation. Remember Negative Nigel or Negative Nancy and Positive Patricia or Positive Peter?

Confidence, or lack thereof, plays a large part in procrastination, both at the start and as procrastination takes hold. Confidence and self-management are part of the staple diet of a good manager, and a manager who has these and the want and will as a mainstay will see them reflected in their own performance, their team's performance, and contributing greatly to the business's performance.

Procrastination takes your confidence and gnaws away until there's nothing left except low self-esteem and either a submissive or aggressive communication style to compensate.

You read earlier about the whingeing mindset and the requirement to choose your battles to win the war. Procrastination flies in the face of choosing your battles, internally validating your complaints and feeding the 'bad things always happen to me' attitude. Procrastination does not allow for a mindset that thinks about the solutions required. Possibly even worse, whilst others are working and making an effort to find solutions to the problems, the procrastinator fends off any thoughts in order not to have to face the task in hand.

A manager who procrastinates demotivates their team. Just as bad is a manager who doesn't have the confidence or the time to address procrastinators within his or her team. Procrastination can be an infectious illness within the team and can drain it of any energy, want or will it may have had.

The Step-Up Mindset takes the tools within this book to counteract procrastination and puts in place a plan that energises, motivates and influences self and others to face the task in hand. It recognises and acknowledges procrastination and then kicks it into touch.

Time management is up there with procrastination in terms of the most debilitating thing that stops a manager in their tracks. Understand what is important and what is urgent versus who's shouting the loudest, although there is obviously a need to take into account the VIPs or senior individuals requesting something from you.

Let's begin with first things first.

DELEGATION

Delegation can be an uncomfortable subject. It will not be once you think through the process.

It is a priority for new managers to start implementing and feeling comfortable with delegation. Let's understand who can be delegates as well as what should be delegated, and what cannot be delegated.

There aren't many new managers in existence who particularly enjoy delegation. Most find it a hard pill to swallow. This can be due to the fact that they don't know how to delegate, and this is the same for some more senior managers. They feel that by delegating they are giving up their power to others.

Good managers work towards making themselves redundant from their role, and this is mainly achieved through great delegation. The very thought of this may scare you, but note that I said from the *role* and not from the *company*. Working towards making yourself redundant from your role should be seen as a positive, part of the Step-Up Mindset phase, and it may look something like this:

A good manager prepares for their next role by delivering at a higher than required level within their current role and showing great potential for their next move. If you become indispensable within your role, how will you possibly be promoted? If you are doing everything yourself, how will you show your potential and climb the career ladder?

You get promoted on potential, paid on performance.

Delegation is not about giving up control. It's not about handing over your power to another, or giving up responsibility or ownership. Delegation is about sharing the workload, challenging and growing your team, freeing up your time to manage, showing the team that you trust them and allowing you to assess strengths and areas that require improvement. This will allow you to manage not only your own time, but also your team's time more effectively. Effective time management is a core skill for a good manager with the Step-Up Mindset.

Time stealers

Time stealers are the enemy of any good manager – of any individual, for that matter. They are people who continuously interrupt you by walking up to your desk expecting instant responses; phone up asking obvious questions; put invites in your calendar without any agenda or obvious reason for you to be there. Time stealers always copy you in on emails that are irrelevant to you, covering their own backsides.

Tasks can also be time stealers, for example the email notifications that pop up when you are working on something and cause you to stop and check on them; tasks you've allocated a period of time that take so much longer and steal time from another task; tasks you procrastinate about starting or completing; tasks you really enjoy working on so you drag out the fun and ignore other essential tasks.

Time stealers must be dealt with assertively – remember win/win.

Emails

Emails are one of life's greatest time stealers. I would say from personal experience that 95% of people respond to email notifications as soon as the notification appears on the computer. Between marketing emails, unsolicited emails, emails that you have been CCed into, and no response required emails, I would hazard a guess that 80% of emails coming through your inbox do not need to be actioned or even read. They make no impact on your day to day working, nor do they work towards anything productive.

Meetings

And now we are talking about one of business's biggest resource drains. Ladies and gentlemen, I give you (drum roll please): *meetings*.

As a manager you will experience the phenomenon that is meetings. What a drain on time, money and energy these become if not managed correctly – they are up there with emails. I am amazed at the amount of time people spend arranging meetings, holding meetings, and then... nothing!

Meetings often require a lot of people 'just in case', and then there is chaos within the room. Time is spent over the pettiest of points, and larger points are then rushed through. Individuals walk away from the meeting questioning its validity. Then they attend the next one and carry out the same cycle over and over again. Why the madness? (*The definition of insanity is doing something over and over again and expecting a different result.* – Albert Einstein) Why the repeated waste of resources? Why is this allowed to happen?

Everyone gets caught up in the cycle, and with heavy workloads and dismal time management, it feels like too much to take on to step out of the cycle and think it through. It is easier to go with the flow and not push against it.

The 'Bike Shed Effect'

Parkinson's Law of Triviality is also known as the Bike Shed Effect. It is based around an imaginary management meeting where the committee comes together to discuss nuclear plant plans and other smaller matters. The nuclear plant plans are passed over within minutes, but one of the minor matters, the colour of the bike shed, is discussed for hours i.e., the committee's focus and time is spent on the more trivial item, with minimal time spent on the important item.

Is this due to lack of understanding or knowledge of the subject? For whatever reason, this continues to be the case today. The outcome of these meetings often results in wasted time and energy, demoralising feelings, and detracts from the important issues that have a positive impact on business growth. And yet, the Bike Shed Effect continues to focus attendees on the little things and gloss over the important issues.

Why are managers not owning this? Are they enablers? Is there a culture within *your* business that silently promotes this? *Qui tacet consentit* – silence gives consent.

Parkinson is also quoted as having said that work expands to fill the time available.

MANAGING TIME STEALERS

Interrupting callers

There will be times when a caller has an urgent request which must be dealt with. However, do not become the 'go to' person for others who are not managing their time. When you receive either a desk visit or a phone call and you are in the middle of something urgent, or recognise that you have a repeat offender, the situation has to be dealt with assertively.

Ask the individual to call or drop by at a later time, giving them the time to return, "I am free at 16.00, can we discuss it then?"

By setting expectations, you will find that people (over time) get used to your way of working and become more considerate. You will also find that people (particularly your team) will start to find out the answers for themselves. This action alone will save you time.

Emails

One of the first things to do is switch off *all* message arrival alerts on your email system. This way you will check email when you are ready and not when the system alerts you to incoming mail. Ensure that you cancel all message arrival alerts on your mobile devices too.

Schedule into your calendar times in the day to go to your inbox and deal with the emails. These times must be when you are able to give the emails your full attention and not when you are in the middle of carrying out a task. Never start working on both a task and emails as you'll give neither your best.

Stop the madness that is dependency on emails and the need to measure your importance on the number of emails received.

I hear you screaming, "You wrote earlier in the book about responsiveness and holding emails, now you are saying not to respond immediately. Make your mind up!"

To clarify, I am saying that you *choose* when to check your emails. You check them when you have the time and mental space to deal with them.

Effective meetings

I am absolutely an advocate of new managers getting as much knowledge of the business as they can, within reason. Attending meetings is one avenue to carry out this knowledge gathering, and another is networking, covered earlier in the book. However, there will come a time when the meetings are no longer useful, and at this time you will want to start managing the value of them.

If you are chairing a meeting, ensure that you:

- Have an obvious first point, an agenda. Allocate timings for each agenda item.

- Set the scene for each agenda item *before* the individual discussion, e.g. say, "I know that this is a bone of contention, but we have 10 minutes to come up with an answer. Please write down your solution, then let's go with the majority vote and move on to the next item."

- Ensure that the important tasks are at the beginning of the meeting. If the meeting does over run, the less important tasks can roll over to the next meeting.

- If an item rolls over more than twice, drop it from the agenda. It is not important.

- When an agenda item is being offered for the meeting, ask the contributor what the objective of the item is. Be very clear with the objective: it will allow you to direct the conversation back if it goes off track.

- Finish the meeting on or before time, never finish a meeting late. Respect others' time.

If you are not chairing the meeting, request an agenda and ask the chairperson what they would like from your attendance. This way you can prepare, and if your input and output is minimal you can request a first or last slot. That way you do not need to sit through the whole meeting for a couple of minutes' input.

This approach may be alien to you and your company, but what will happen once it is seen to be working is it will become second nature to you and part of the company culture.

Essentials versus desirables

Another great time waster is choosing to carrying out tasks that you enjoy doing, often at the expense of essentials. However, in fairness to most managers they do not have a clear idea of what is essential and what is desirable and two of the key areas that we're looking at in this chapter are essentials and desirables.

It is important to note at this point that desirables for yourself and your team are often the motivators behind performance. It is crucial to know and understand what these desirables are. And, it is essential that as a manager you understand when desirables are put first with non tangible returns on investment to the team or the business, whilst the essential tasks are being put on the back burner.

Part of understanding when a task is essential and when it's desirable is having a good understanding of the time involved in the task. The exercise highlighted in the following story is crucial to carry out when considering time management. Not only does it take into account and give you better control and management over essential tasks versus desirable tasks, it also gives you greater understanding of where your own time and your team's time has been spent.

The non-accounts accounts assistant

When I was carrying out a customer service programme for a large construction company, one of the exercises was for the individuals to list their key tasks, and alongside note the percentage of their working week spent on each task. One guest highlighted one key task that would take 35% of his working week. This task was to chase invoice payments, the aim being to ensure that the team could continue to place orders for equipment required for the business to continue working. Surprised by the task, I asked if his job responsibilities were directly connected with accounts.

He responded, "No, I don't work for accounts."

His manager, who was in attendance at the same workshop, was surprised. At the break, the manager and the guest went away to discuss the merits of this task, and on returning the guest shared with the group that his manager and himself had come to the conclusion that over a third of his working week was spent doing someone else's job. Whilst it is vital that invoices get paid, if accounts ran the service and the plant team ensured the process was adhered to, this would reduce that individual's work by 35%.

As a direct result of this exercise, the guest and his manager arranged a meeting to hand back this particular task to accounts. Seven days later the guest had stopped chasing invoices and was focusing on scheduling his time towards more productive tasks.

Areas that must be considered when looking to change your attitude and outcomes on time management are:

- scheduling and prioritising work;

- essential versus desirable tasks;

- delegation;

- goal setting.

Schedule and prioritise

Scheduling and prioritising your work will release so much time. It will also give you the confidence to set realistic deadlines (remember – under-promise and over-deliver) and push back when asked to cover someone else's emergency.

When receiving a task, assist in scheduling and prioritising by considering where it fits into the scheme of work using the following questions:

- Does this task need to be carried out?

- Does it need to be done now or later?

- Does it need to be done by myself or someone else?

To get the answers to these, consider the importance and urgency of the task. Important and urgent must be defined within the role and to you.

I find this particularly helpful when dealing with large volumes of emails, verbal requests and tasks.

Importance

- Is this task important to my role and myself?

- Will it work towards meeting my own and my company's goals? (Of course, I am assuming you know your company's goals.)

- What impact will this task have on my company?

- Will it drive my department's success forward?

Urgency

- What is the deadline for this task?

- How will it impact my role if the deadline is/is not met?

- How will it impact my department's and company's role if the deadline is/is not met?

Once you have clear definitions of important and urgent, apply the following AC/DC methodology to the task.

AC/DC TO SCHEDULING AND PRIORITISING

AC/DC in electrical terms means **A**lternating **C**urrent/ **D**irect **C**urrent, which is a process of flow and direction for electricity. Within self-management, we use AC/DC to manage the flow and direction of time. Using AC/DC is a great way of considering the task and how to schedule and prioritise it, allowing you to flow and where necessary change current and direction.

AC/DC for us means **A**ction, **C**alendar, **D**elegate and **C**ancel. Once you are familiar with the thinking around important and urgent, you will find that you will be able to apply the AC/DC methodology very quickly – it often takes a second or less for me to apply it to my emails, though it did take me a short time to create the habit of always applying the methodology and thinking through the important and urgent process. (I used the old fashioned handwritten note taped to my screen as a reminder.)

The following breaks down AC/DC.

Important and urgent – action

If a task has to be carried out by you (important) and carried out quickly (urgent), I would suggest that the action falls into a same day or first thing tomorrow category.

Important not urgent – calendar

If a task has to be carried out by you (important) and carried out at a later date (not urgent), it should immediately be transferred to your calendar. Once you have carried this out, you can then forget about it until the date arrives.

Not important and urgent – delegate

If a task can be delegated to someone else (not important to you) but needs to be carried out by them quickly (urgent), it should immediately be tasked to them (see end of chapter for the process on delegating tasks). Once you have carried this out, you can then relax, knowing the task is being dealt with.

Not important and not urgent – cancel

If a task is not important and not urgent, it can be cancelled out, but before cancelling and deleting it, ensure that it is not meant for someone else. If it should be delegated, delegate it.

If the task is in an email, delete it. If it is a piece of paper, recycle it. If it is a verbal request, say no and suggest the requester looks elsewhere. Think assertively (win/win) when saying no. Your win is you are not carrying out someone else's role and therefore can get on with your own work; the requester's win is they are potentially getting the right person to carry out the task.

Action

If, like me, you tend to receive the majority of task requests by email, there is a tendency to hold them within your inbox until you do something (anything) with them. Being faced with a large volume of emails can often feel overwhelming, so a great habit is to aim to reduce your email inbox to a minimum amount of emails. This may mean that your inbox only holds your actionable emails. All other emails are placed elsewhere.

After deciding that a task is important and urgent, therefore requiring a quick response, mark an A (for action) alongside the email. When applying the AC/DC methodology to your tasks, the A will imply that you intend to work on the task quickly (that being within the next 24 hours). Therefore, your email should remain in your inbox until you action and deal with it.

When actioning an email or task, ensure you keep it somewhere prominent and easy to access.

If you deem the task urgent – action, you will want to consider the time available to carry it out. If it is a quick task, you may want to keep it and other quick tasks together and work on them at the same time.

Email allocated time slots

I have three recurring half hour slots allocated in my daily calendar, and a fourth of an hour. These times are set aside to check emails and work on the quick (5–10 minute) action responses. If a task will only take a minute or two to complete, it is often worthwhile carrying the task out there and then to completion.

Yep, you read that right: I check my emails four times a day and have turned off the pop-up alerts within my email system to stop the interruptions. Email was a big time stealer for me, so now I manage when I check emails and do not allow myself to be dragged in by the alerts. This means when I am working on a task, it generally receives my full uninterrupted attention.

The above action task methodology may also be applied to other forms of requests, verbal or written.

Calendar

Now you are moving on to tasks that are to be completed by you but they do not require immediate attention. When deciding that a task is important and not urgent, mark a C (for calendar) alongside it.

Your calendar is your lifeline to time management, the bible from which you work. When you assign the category of calendar from the AC/DC methodology, you must think through the time involved in completing the task. Can it be completed in one sitting? If yes, how much time must you put aside? If no, how many sittings and how long will each be?

Extending your calendar

If you have a task to do, it should be in your calendar. It is irrelevant where the task originated from – if you have agreed to carry something out at a later date, place it in the calendar. Large tasks should be broken down into smaller steps and the times required placed alongside each step in your calendar. Blocking out the time in smaller chunks should make the task less overwhelming, and dedicating separate times will give you breathing space should emergencies crop up.

As with smaller tasks in action, you may wish to assign other small tasks to your allocated times, though remember if it is not urgent, it can be slotted in at a later date.

Point to note: your calendar should include allocated time slots for all tasks, meetings, travel, lunch, etc.

Meetings

Meetings, including travel time, must be in your calendar with reminders. Include separately, if need be, the time to prepare for and after your meeting.

If using an electronic calendar, you can set up reminders in advance of the meeting. This is a great feature.

Buffer time

You must allow buffer time for the unknown, the time stealers, the emergencies and the changing deadlines. Buffer time will give you the breathing space required when the ugly stuff hits the fan.

Placing your future tasks in the calendar gives you the confidence to let go of recurring thoughts or worries regarding the task. You can take confidence from the fact you have thought through the task and assigned it a date or dates for completion.

DELEGATING TASKS

Delegate

Delegation is such an important part of the manager's role. It is level in importance with communication.

When carried out correctly, delegation can be liberating not just for you as a manager, but also for your team. It really does feed the trust between you and your team, which grows your reputation and brand.

When you decide that a task is not important but it is urgent, it requires you to delegate. Mark a D (for delegation) alongside the task.

Having a solid process in place to deal with delegation is vital, and there are key steps that need to be considered. Working through these will give you peace of mind that you are remaining in control, have set the correct standards within the correct time limits and the task has been thought through.

1. Can the task be delegated?

2. Should the task be delegated?

3. Who is best suited to carrying out the task?

4. Set defined outcomes

5. Set deadlines

6. Allow buffer times

7. Agree times for progress updates

8. Support delegate

9. Recognise and reward good work

Always when delegating, I mentally run through the process (appendices) then follow this up by using the TRUST template. I often hand over the completed TRUST template to the delegate after discussing the task with them and garnering their buy-in, using steps and target dates as progress points.

If these are set as meetings, it is crucial that the meetings are adhered to. Don't find other things to do as this will undermine the importance of the task for your team member. Milestones must be checked and recognition given for good work, or feedback and support to get the delegate back on track if the task is not completed as per your schedule or to the agreed standard.

Cancel

Quite simply put, if a task is not important or urgent to you, cancel it out.

When you've decided that a task is not important or urgent, mark an X (for cancel) alongside it.

You will get to a place where you do not even have to mark the task with the assigned outcome as it will become very natural. In fact, when it comes to cancelling, I would always just delete the task without marking it with an X.

DAILY TO DO LISTS

Oh, the joy of to do lists. I can almost feel you rolling your eyes when you think of them. However, if carried out correctly, they work. They really do.

At the very worst, to do lists are great for moving all the things that need to be carried out from your head on to paper. This leaves room for you to think through how you are going to carry them out, or for those of you who like to worry, it gives you space to fill with other things.

When you are working on your to do lists, you will get so much more than a clear head. Once you have listed everything, including the personal tasks and errands, you can think through what comes next.

One thing to keep in mind is that your to do list will rarely, if ever, be empty. If it was, what would you be employed to carry out?

WORKING WITH AC/DC

Now to put it into practice.

As you work through your emails, to do list or verbal requests, think:

- Important and urgent – action. If yes, mark an A (for action) alongside the task.

- Important not urgent – calendar. If yes, mark an C (for calendar) alongside the task.

- Not important and urgent – delegate. If yes, mark an D (for delegate) alongside the task.

- Not important and not urgent – cancel. If yes, mark an X (for cancel) alongside the task.

Now you know what your priorities are, you can delete all your Xs. Delegate all your Ds, ideally using your electronic task system, place all your Cs in the calendar and list all your As. With a clear picture of what is priority, you can schedule it. If, like me, you find that your list is long, you need to take this a step further. A good rule of thumb is to break down your essentials from desirables.

One further step for listing you As: this is your to do list. You need to recognise which of these will bring the most return on investment.

Essentials vs desirables

The first thing to consider is: are the tasks essential or desirable? Often when looking down a to do list, you will be tempted to pick out the desirables. After all, your why is stronger and easier to think about than essential tasks. And whilst desirables are great for motivation, they are not so strong on driving the department or the business forward.

Essentials will drive your department as well as the company forward. I suspect you will also have a greater feeling of accomplishment on completing them.

Questions to ask when considering if a task is essential or desirable:

- What is the objective of this task? Is there a clear aim and objective that is tangible?

- What impact will this task have on completion?

- If I were not to carry this task out, would it impact the business greatly? If the answer is yes, it is an essential task; if no, it is a desirable task.

- If I were not to carry this task out, would it impact any one or any other department? If the answer is yes, it is an essential task; if no, it is a desirable task.

- If I were not to carry this task out, would anyone miss it? If the answer is yes, it is an essential task; if no, it is a desirable task.

- Who benefits most from the completion of this task?

The above questions are based on the premise that you have carried out the AC/DC methodology on the task.

Once you have a clearer understanding of essential and desirable tasks, they must be prioritised. What are the top three tasks that must be completed?

Now consider splitting your day into 3 segments:

- Segment one – start time until 11.30

- Segment two – 11.30 until 14.30

- Segment three – 14.30 until close of play

Keep in mind your other calendar commitments when applying this rule of thumb. If your task is in the top 3 and is actually the top one, assuming it has to be completed by 11.30, assign a 1 to it. If task 2 has to be completed by 14.30, assign a 2 to it, and if task 3 also has to be completed by 14.30 assign a 2 to it. Other tasks to be completed by close of play can have a 3 alongside them.

Point to note: this can be tied in with the task audits from Chapter 8.

Return on investment

By carrying out the above steps you will find that you spend your time on the top 3 priorities, and you and your department will be delivering. Having the time to complete the further tasks adds to productivity.

What a great place to be.

Team time management

Team numbers I suspect will depend on the budget allocation. Your team's delivery will reflect on you and your reputation, so it is imperative to have a way of managing the team's deadlines as a whole. I am not for one second suggesting that you carry this out at a micromanaging stage; there are more productive ways to do this, and there is plenty of software in the market that will make it easier.

I tend to keep it simple, and have found that an Excel Workbook has worked for me in the past.

Task	Owner	Progress %	Start Date	Completion Date	RAG	TRUST #
ABC Report	MM	25	01/01/15	15/05/15	Red	5
Software Process	JDS	90	05/10/15	31/12/15	Amber	11
Team Building Day	RP	75	31/10/15	28/02/16	Green	32

The 'Task' column is the task being managed, 'Owner' is who is responsible and has accepted ownership of the task and 'Progress' shows percentage completed. Start date is self-explanatory, and completion date is the hard deadline for completion.

The RAG column is the traffic light system: red, amber and green. This is generally a visual representation of the task's status. Red – there is a strong possibility of non-delivery. Amber – there is a real need to rethink the task and timings as the task is behind schedule. Green – all is on track.

The final column, TRUST#, is the TRUST form that the task pertains too. Remember that when others are involved in a task, there is a need to use TRUST in order to be clear on requirements and stakeholders.

And finally, on the topic of time management, this is a learnt habit: a behaviour that can be fine-tuned. It is also a key area that many managers, and actually people in general, are measured on.

What do you want people to think of you when it comes to time management?

CHAPTER REFLECTION AND ACTION – MANAGING YOUR TIME

Disciplined

If you are disciplined with your time and that of your team, you will find that both your and your team's productivity will increase greatly. Not only that, stress levels will decrease, confidence will grow, as will your and your department's reputation. Managing time stealers, kicking procrastination's butt, applying AC/DC and delegating will lead to a more proficient mindset.

Procrastination process

1. Stop and breathe. No need to panic or feel bad. You are now taking control.

2. On your own, write down a list of tasks and actions that you need to carry out. Keep your list handy as things will pop up and you can add to it as you go along.

3. Choose the appropriate TRUST form. Now complete a form for each task that needs breaking down. If you're wondering if a task needs breaking down, then it does.

4. Reward yourself, although I imagine you are feeling so much better already as you are taking control.

Time stealers

Working with the Daily Time Log and Analysis, find out who or what are your time stealers.

As you work through your day, each time you start a new task, place this against the time on the form. As you are interrupted or choose to distract yourself from the task, place a note of this alongside the task.

After a week, you will start to see a trend of who or what is stealing your time. Repeat this for two weeks, review your findings and implement a plan to banish the time stealers.

Delegation process

The following process is a physical starter. As with all processes in this book, it is not meant to be followed rigidly step by step if not all the steps work for you. See them as a starting point for you to add to or delete, and make the process your own.

- How often do I carry out this task?

- Can the task be delegated?

- Should the task be delegated?

- Who is best suited to carrying out the task?

    o What will they learn from carrying out this task?

    o Will they be motivated to carry it out to the best of their ability, and to my standards?

- Am I clear about the outcomes of this task?

- Am I clear about the deadlines for this task?

- What development will be required by the delegates to complete this task?

- When is it best to meet to discuss the progress of the task?

- How often should we meet to discuss the progress of the task?

DAILY TIME LOG AND ANALYSIS

Date: Day:

Time	Task	1	2	3	4	5	6	7	8	9	10
08:00											
08:30											
09:00											
09:30											
10:00											
10:30											
11:00											
11:30											
12:00											
12:30											
13:00											
13:30											
14:00											
14:30											
15:00											
15:30											
16:00											
16:30											
17:00											
17:30											

BOOK REFLECTION AND ACTION

The Way Forward

This book is not about making you a manager who can talk a good game with theories and methodologies. It is all about ensuring you can deliver, and deliver well.

Managers are human and will make mistakes, and that is OK. The great point of making mistakes is that you learn from them and aim not to repeat them.

There will be a high possibility that your to do list will never be empty, and that's good. It means that you are always striving for more. An empty to do list should worry you.

Having completed the book, stop and breathe. You aim is not to carry out all the action points at once, that is way too much to take on in one sitting. Instead, work through the following:

1. Which three tasks can you implement that will give you quick wins? What will stop you implementing these? What can you do to resolve these issues?

2. Which three tasks can you implement that will have a big impact on the outcomes? What will stop you implementing these? What can you do to resolve these issues?

3. Which three tasks can you implement that will have long lasting impact? What will stop you implementing these? What can you do to resolve these issues?

Consider taking one task from each of the three questions above. Now is the time to take real action and apply your Step-Up Mindset to becoming a great manager.

RESOURCES AND REFERENCES

Simon Sinek, *Start With Why*, 2009

Les Enfants Terribles, *Alice in Wonderland*, 2015

ABOUT THE AUTHOR

Margo Manning has worked in the development arena for 25+ years. In the last 15 years, Margo has been delivering as one of the UK's top Leadership and Management Coaches and Facilitators.

Margo is the architect of the 3:2 Management Model and subsequent 3:2 Management Development Programme that is delivered and adopted within many businesses, large and small, nationally and internationally. She has worked, and continues to work, with new mangers through to senior managers in companies such as Goldman Sachs, Hobart Lovells, Brunswick Group, Tower Hamlets Homes, Aon, Balfour Beatty, Kantar, and many more.

As a first time author, Margo's focus wholly remains with her passion: people development.